Small Talk

A Practical Guide to Improve Your Conversations

(Learn the Secret to Building Genuine Connections in Achieving Your Life Goals)

Daniel Jordan

I0519061

Published By **Kate Sanders**

Daniel Jordan

Small Talk: A Practical Guide to Improve Your Conversations (Learn the Secret to Building Genuine Connections in Achieving Your Life Goals)

ISBN   978-1-9991564-7-3

Legal & Disclaimer

Table Of Contents

Chapter 1: Mastering The Art Work Of Icebreakers

Be Authentic: When it consists of icebreakers, authenticity is actually vital. People are normally capable of stumble on whether or not or no longer or no longer you are being disingenuous or in case you are using pre-written comments Instead, placed your electricity into being yourself and expressing actual hobby inside the human beings round you. It is beneficial to extend a relationship with a person based on consider and authenticity in case you percentage non-public memories or evaluations which can be right to who you are as someone.

Smiling and supplying a nice frame language may additionally brief placed people snug and lead them to revel in extra at home whilst you're inside the identical room with them. It gives the have an effect on which you are approachable and great. Maintaining eye contact, sitting or reputation up instantly, and no longer crossing your fingers are all critical even as having a communicate because of the fact those moves may also moreover assemble partitions and make it tough to have a verbal exchange.

Keep things light and amusing: The cause of icebreakers is to interrupt the ice and assist people feel greater cushty in their surroundings. If you want to foster an surroundings this is mild-hearted and exquisite for each person, strive on the aspect of some funny or a laugh additives into the questions or sports you advocate. Developing a feel of rapport and overcoming boundaries might be facilitated via laughter and fantastic upbeat feelings.

It is important to don't forget that numerous cultures have severa necessities and sensitivities, therefore it's miles vital to appreciate these variations. When utilizing icebreakers, it's far important to be aware about the possibility for cultural versions. This will help you prevent via threat frightening or setting aside everybody. Avoid asking inquiries that even remotely contact on concern topics like faith, politics, non-public opinions, or awesome potentially sensitive subjects.

Beginning with What You Have in Common With human beings Discovering what you have in commonplace with people is an powerful method to connect with them. Start up with a few icebreakers that concentrate on the revel in or placing that everyone has had in commonplace. For example, if you are going to a conference, you must inquire approximately the speaker or the state of affairs this is going to be protected. Beginning with scenario matters which may be already famous to contributors creates a sense of kinship and makes it much less complex to start discussions.

Make Use of Open-Ended Questions: Open-ended questions are superior than closed-ended questions, which fine elicit easy "positive" or "no" replies. Open-ended questions entice extra massive and thrilling responses from the respondent. Asking questions that start with "how," "what," or "why" can elicit practical replies from the listener and open the door for precise opportunities to discover the difficulty. This approach allows for delivered considerable talks to take region at the equal time as additionally fostering deeper ties amongst people.

First, Share: Setting an instance for others to have a examine might possibly make it easier for others to open up and talk their very personal perspectives, reviews, and perspectives. Before asking others to do the equal, you want to break the ice with the aid of providing a honest solution or sharing a few factor approximately yourself on the identical time as the use of an icebreaker. This motion fosters a feeling of reciprocity and encourages human beings to percentage their mind and emotions.

Listen cautiously to others :When taking part in talks that have been started by using manner of using icebreakers, attentive listening may be very important. Maintain eye touch, actively pay attention to what wonderful human beings have to mention, and bring which you are interested in what they've to say. Consider their remarks and come up with some considerate look at-up questions to expose that you respect what they have got to say. This diploma of recognition creates deeper involvement and allows to enhance present relationships.

Include everyone: The icebreakers you use want to be open to anyone and take their consolation stage into interest. Steer easy of asking people questions that could make them feel awkward or exposed, which consist of the ones concerning personal or sensitive subjects such as their cash, fitness, or courting popularity. Make positive that your icebreakers are open to every person and may be tailored to in shape the dreams of a huge sort of contributors.

Prepare in Advance: If you be given as actual with that you will be in a putting in which icebreakers can be beneficial, it is a exceptional idea to spend a while in advance preparing some questions or communique openers to use in the setting. This steering allows you to experience greater secure and ensures which you have relevant and interesting icebreakers organized to head every time the occasion provides itself to apply them.

Adapt the Icebreakers to the Situation: When selecting icebreakers for a assembly, it is essential to recall the specific placing similarly to the reason for the collection. Different contexts call for using unique techniques. For instance, the icebreakers played at a laid-lower back occasion might be very remarkable from those executed at a professional convention. You also can furthermore help expand a connection that is extra considerable and applicable to the scenario by way of the usage of adapting your icebreakers to match the surroundings.

Encourage Participation: If you're in rate of a fixed or are moderating a communique, it is essential that you do all for your energy to get others worried. Establish a putting that is warmth and accepting, one this is with out judgment, and one which inspires people to revel in snug whilst expressing their thoughts. Recognizing and appreciating the contributions made with the useful resource of each character member of the institution will assist to domesticate a feel of inclusiveness and involvement some of the participants of the business enterprise.

Steer clean of Using the Same Questions Over and Over Again Questions which can be used regularly as icebreakers can also additionally get antique and predictable. If you want to hold subjects exciting and new, try and bear in mind a few creative icebreakers so one can pique people's hobby and elicit reactions which can be all their private. Conversations can be made extra exciting and high-quality with using questions which might be novel and surprising.

Recognize When It's Time to Move On: Not each attempt at breaking the ice gets the response that became desired or reason a lively communicate. It is critical to evaluate the events and function a flexible attitude. In the occasion that an icebreaker appears to be unsuccessful or drags on for too prolonged without generating the essential diploma of participation, you need to smoothly segue to each other difficulty or activity as a way to maintain the go with the flow of power.

Exercise Empathy: Being empathetic is one of the most crucial talents for breaking the ice efficiently. Put yourself in the function of the opposite character and bear in mind how they ought to be feeling and what they need to be going thru. Pay interest to their responses, and alter your technique in moderate of what you studies from them. By demonstrating empathy, you are able to hook up with others on a deeper diploma, and also you moreover create a solid surroundings wherein significant dialogues can also moreover take place.

Keep in mind that the cause of icebreakers is to establish a pleasant and comfortable surroundings in which individuals can also moreover feel extra comfortable and take part more actively in the communicate. You turns into extra professional at mastering the art work of icebreakers in case you exercise and supply careful interest to the surroundings in that you are doing the challenge.

Effective ice breaking strategies

Icebreakers are strong equipment that can be used to start discussions and make relationships with splendid people. Let's have a have a have a look at a few actual-international eventualities and illustrative examples that show a way to end up an expert inside the artwork of icebreakers:

The Event Icebreaker: Let's say you're at a networking occasion and also you see someone status via the usage of themselves. What ought to you're announcing to them? Approach them with a welcoming grin and start a communication thru developing a comic story at the occasion itself to interrupt the ice. You may additionally begin through manner of greeting anybody and remarking, "Hello, I noticed there are such an entire lot of interesting speakers protected up to speak in recent times." Is there a excessive exceptional presentation that you're searching ahead to the maximum? The person you approached reciprocated with an real and heartfelt smile, conveying their honest gratitude in a truly first-rate manner. They react with "Oh, most clearly!" The upcoming communicate on effective control strategies has piqued my interest masses. Recently, I've had a whole lot of problem dealing with it on my own employer. Where do you stand? I changed into wondering whether or no longer there has been a specific issue that piqued your hobby.

You and this exclusive person have a shared hobby in leadership, so that you strike up a speak about it and talk approximately the significance of strong management in present day current-day place of business. As you preserve to speak, you every find out which you have faced similar problems and professional comparable situations at the same time as primary agencies. The icebreaker did its interest properly and cleared the course for a sizable verbal exchange, to be able to allow you to percentage your perspectives and advantage from each special's lifestyles reports.

The icebreaker at the occasion not best helped you connect with a person but also gave you the opportunity to move in addition into a subject that have become of hobby to both of you. You set the tone for a snug and alluring surroundings for conversation with the aid of setting up with a honest comment on the prevalence, which paved the manner for others to sign up for in. This approach of breaking the ice may be carried out in loads of networking activities, conferences, or business enterprise gatherings in which the attendees have a shared hobby or goal.

Keep in thoughts that being attentive to the alternative individual, cautiously paying attention to their feedback, after which increasing upon what they said are all crucial components of effective icebreakers. It is viable to have a closer speak with another individual by the usage of asking them open-ended questions, which additionally encourages the opportunity character to provide their issue of view. You might also furthermore installation a pleasing and attractive speak this is going past the floor diploma of small chat with the resource of showing a real hobby in the exceptional man or woman's reviews.

This e-book digs further into the art work of occasion icebreakers, giving additional strategies and real-existence examples to help you draw close the talents of starting conversations at networking sports and building huge connections that might open doorways to new possibilities. You can find out "The Science of Small Talk" absolutely on

Amazon.Com, supplying a uniquely reachable platform to discover and purchase the book.

The Observation Icebreaker: Let's say you are standing in line at your favorite espresso preserve even as you appearance over and spot the individual in the front of you analyzing a e-book written thru clearly definitely one of your all-time favored authors. Share a number of your mind on it to function a conversation starter. It may be OK for you to say some detail along the strains of, "I couldn't assist but phrase which you're analyzing [Dr. Steve S. Christian]. Your assertion inspires a pleasing response from the individual you engaged with, inflicting them to raise their eyes from the e-book, carrying a especially pleased expression. "Their novels are certainly tremendous in each viable way!" I'm curious, which one do you find out yourself the usage of the maximum? They offer a type grin and observation something to the effect of, "Oh, it's miles great to fulfill some other fan!" Currently, I'm making my way through Dr.

Steve S. Christian's ebook titled "The Art of Meaningful Conversations." His observations and thoughts on communique are pretty thrilling to me. Have you have a look at any of the alternative subjects that he has written?

You maintain the conversation thru presenting the ebook written with the useful useful resource of Dr. Steve S. Christian that you remember to be your all-time preferred and bringing interest to the impact that Dr. Christian's extraordinary writings have had to your private potential to talk without a doubt. You speak to each different and offer each different terms of information and insights, delving in addition into the nuances of effective communication and the value of having enormous conversations in the international that we live in today with its frenetic pace.

Not fine did the declaration icebreaker kick off a communication, but it additionally induced the formation of a direct bond due to the individuals' shared enthusiasm for a sure author. This happened due to the fact that each businesses had read works written via the usage of manner of the identical creator. By displaying your actual enthusiasm for the reading fabric that they've decided on, you have created a issue of connection with the other individual, which has made it possible for a verbal exchange to go beyond the primary statement and right into a higher communicate.

Icebreakers which can be oriented on making observations carry out specially nicely in comfortable places like as coffee stores, ready rooms, or public transportation. These varieties of settings lend itself to a more open and fine disposition. They make it smooth to begin conversations with not unusual strangers primarily based on some thing inside the surrounding environment that you and the alternative individual have seen, that's a extremely good way to fulfill new humans. The use of observations as icebreakers can also additionally moreover reason fascinating talks, that may then bring about the identification of pastimes which can be shared with the aid of the individuals. These comments might be made about a e-book, a one-of-a-kind object, or a shocking piece of artwork.

When the use of icebreakers which is probably primarily based mostly on observations, it is critical to keep in thoughts that the pleasant approach to break the ice is to expose consideration for the alternative character and to method the difficulty with interest, in vicinity of as an intrusion. Keep an open thoughts approximately what the opportunity character may want to say, and then use what they are announcing as a springboard for extra speak as soon as you've got listened to what they have got to mention. Listening carefully and showing a actual hobby within the mindset of the individual you're speaking with might also help to assemble a great communique.

The ebook "The Science of Small Talk" provides you with further ideas and examples of announcement-based totally icebreakers, which offers you the potential to provoke conversations pretty actually in some of regular instances. If you grasp the artwork of commentary icebreakers, you'll be in a role to show smooth observations into thrilling connections and open the door to opportunities for having exquisite discussions. Because of this, you may have the capability to show observations into a few factor extra.

The Accumulated Reflections of Everyone: Imagine which you are attending a session that is supposed to hold humans together to create teams. At this workshop, every body is engaged in a separate hobby. Discuss the shared experience in depth with a distinct character thru utilizing it as a springboard for speak. You may moreover, as an example, assertion some thing along the strains of, "That interest that we simply completed modified into in reality difficult, but it have become moreover fun! I become wondering what your opinions have been at the state of affairs. When you technique them, they smile and nod their head in agreement, as although they may be relieved to have someone else with whom they may talk their experience.Their reaction is an unequivocal affirmation, as they exclaim, "Absolutely, actually! Despite the truth that I need to concede that the interest furnished a large impediment, I am unable to deny that it have end up each an wonderful and wonderful analyzing enjoy. It was uncomfortable for me to transport outdoor of my protection area, but therefore, I picked up lots of new facts. Where do you stand in this debate? How would possibly you in my opinion look at your reviews approximately it, deliberating your thoughts-set?

You and your associate begin a verbal exchange about the hobby that centers on the formation of businesses. During the path of the verbal exchange, you discover the disturbing conditions you confronted, the strategies you used to triumph over those demanding conditions, and the belongings you found out as a right away effect of taking detail within the experience. As you skip similarly into the shared experience, you and the opportunity man or woman find out which you have similar methods and mind, which develops a connection that extends beyond the icebreaker that turn out to be first used.

The shared encounter that each one the ones concerned had You might also additionally use a previous event or hobby that you and particular people have participated in as a element of reference to each other if you use an icebreaker to help clean the approach.

The Use of Humor as an Icebreaker: Depending at the putting, humor can be an super manner to break the ice. Let's don't forget you are at a party and you see someone who is sporting an thrilling object. What must you do? You should probable destroy the ice with a light-hearted assertion which include, "I ought to mention, your hat most absolutely gives the gathering with a chunk of aptitude! Where on this planet did you get it?

When you're making a humorous statement, the person you approach responds with a chuckle, showing that they rate your sense of humor. Their response is "Thank you plenty! This wonderful hat exudes an unparalleled enchantment, acting as my covert tool for imbuing each gathering with thrill and transmuting it into an indelible affair. It turned into in reality in a antique boutique downtown wherein I befell to find out it with the aid of twist of fate. Should you discover yourself inside the network at any element, they have a few surprises in hold for you.

The tone of the dialogue is set up to be mild and funny way to this witty icebreaker. You every snicker on the equal comedian tale, and from that aspect on, the speak simply flows with out troubles. You can also keep the conversation on one-of-a-type discoveries in style, exchange anecdotes approximately reminiscing approximately unforgettable accessories, or maybe check out special hilarious components of the birthday celebration.

Because they foster an environment that is completely satisfied and carefree, funny icebreakers are superb communique openers due to the mood they assist to set up. You also can moreover assist to interrupt down any initial obstacles and growth an fantastic connection with the alternative character by way of manner of which consist of a hint humor into the come across. Laughter is a remarkable manner to benefit this. This demonstrates that you have a moderate-hearted attitude to socializing, which has the capability to put others snug and stimulate greater speak.

Keep in thoughts that it is important to determine the other character's reaction even as using fun icebreakers, and it is also critical to make sure that your comic story is lighter and properly-intentioned. Avoid making any jokes that is probably seen as hurtful or insensitive via listening to the placing and the comfort diploma of the alternative person. The motive of this exercising is to set the degree for a pleasant and cushty surroundings in which the 2 of you could have a effective communicate.

The e-book "The Science of Small Talk" gives extra examples and techniques for making use of comedy as an icebreaker in pretty some one-of-a-kind kinds of social settings. You also can pump extraordinary strength into talks, boom relationships at the manner to last a whole lifestyles, and make social sports more excellent for actually anyone worried in case you turn out to be expert in the art of the use of a laugh icebreakers.

The Icebreaker in the Form of a Personal Fact: Imagine which you have signed up for a path on non-public improvement, and that during the introductions part of this gadget, each player is requested to percent one exciting fact approximately themselves. Make the maximum of this chance to build a courting with extraordinary people by the use of revealing some component interesting about your self. During my teens, I launched right into a tremendous adventure, venturing thru 3 distinct international locations in the span of an insignificant month. The whirlwind of research that unfold out all through this adventure left an indelible mark on my reminiscence. Can you percentage any charming stories or memorable critiques out of your trips?

The artwork of breaking the ice with compliments: Compliments are a extraordinary manner to expose appreciation for a person even as moreover helping to break the ice. Let's take delivery of as true with you're at a party and you see someone who has an great revel in of fashion and you need to praise them. To begin a discussion, provide a reward that is both sincere and specific. For example, you may say some detail like, "I couldn't assist however look at your impeccable fashion experience." Where do you drift for thoughts while placing up your clothes? When you technique the person, they offer you with a pleasant grin and it is obvious that they're glad with the praise you have got were given given them. In gratitude, they specific their heartfelt appreciation, saying, "I surely understand your kind gesture. Thank you so much!" I am thankful to you for your warmth remarks. I get mind for my garb from a massive style of places, inclusive of fashion websites, publications, or maybe people I see dressed on the street. I definitely anticipate that what I put on ought to be capable of deliver some thing about my character. Where do you stand? Do you find any of your garb to be inspired via extraordinary human beings?

As you preserve speaking to every exceptional, the problem of fashion, person senses of style, and the relevance of self-expression via one's preference of clothes comes up in the direction of the trade. Not tremendous has the praise helped harm the ice among us, however it has moreover generated a actual courting based on a comparable passion in fashion. You every communicate approximately your favored designers, share mind, and offer style recommendation, which makes for an interesting and a laugh discussion.

The free icebreaker gives you the opportunity to make a person experience valued and preferred from the very beginning of your interaction with them. You may additionally additionally show your capability to have a take a look at humans and show interest within the specific capabilities they private through complimenting them in a way that is sincere and specific. This terrific approach straight away creates an inviting environment for the communicate and encourages the opposite character to talk approximately their memories and evaluations.

When breaking the ice with praises, it's miles important to hold in thoughts to be actual and to persuade clean of normal comments. Concentrate on a wonderful element of them that draws your eye, which include their fashion revel in, their desire of add-ons, or maybe sincerely how with any luck they bring about about themselves. You will set up a more significant reference to the individual and demonstrate a real hobby in mastering them in case you customise your complement to the specific attributes that they very own.

The e-book "The Science of Small Talk" gives greater direction and examples of the manner compliments may be used as icebreakers in pretty some awesome social settings. You is probably able to begin discussions with warm temperature, make humans revel in preferred, and set the scene for sizable relationships in case you hold close the artwork of providing compliments which can be actual and thoughtful.

Chapter 2: Creating Memorable

Captivating your target marketplace and setting up the tone for a communicate, presentation, or occasion may be achieved with the aid of crafting starting up strains which is probably memorable and exciting. The following are a few hints that would help you in writing introductory sentences that make an effect:

Start with a Question That Makes You Think to start, ask a query that makes humans curious and encourages them to actively participate inside the verbal exchange. Your target marketplace's interest can be piqued with a rhetorical query, a provocative inquiry, or a hypothetical scenario, as an instance.

Consider this: if you can alter one element within the global, what would it now not be and the way may additionally you skip about doing it?

Provide an uncommon or thrilling records or Statistic Related to Your trouble: One manner to get your goal market inquisitive about your issue is to provide a statistic or statistics that is uncommon or thrilling. This technique is terrific for drawing interest to itself and setting up an air of mystery from the very starting.

Were you conscious that a trifling 10% of our mind's big capability is consciously tapped into? Imagine the possibilities if we want to faucet into the last ninety%."

Storytelling is a sturdy device, and one of the best techniques to capture interest and connect with your target market is to tell an exciting story. Begin your dialogue with a quick tale or a personal revel in that is linked to the trouble on hand. Create an photo this is vivid and familiar to your target market so you can deliver them into the tale. See, The profound impact of finding oneself disoriented in an weird metropolis, with none method to talk within the local language, left a long-lasting have an effect on on my being, underscoring the maximum importance of proficient verbal exchange and the significance of kindness as a giant language."

Use Humor: The use of humor has the power to speedy brighten the mood and establish a brilliant reference to the goal market. Start with a humorous story, story, or humorous observation this is applicable to the problem you are discussing or the occasion this is taking location.

Have you ever contemplated the notion that component is equated to money, best to find yourself in a situation in which you try to settle your payments with a hard and fast of clock arms? Trust me, it does no longer art work!"

Make a Statement That, Challenging Conventional Thinking Employ a provocative assertion with the useful resource of making a observation that is each formidable or arguable and that disturbing conditions conventional thinking. This method has the capacity to stimulate questioning and sell participation out of your aim market.

An instance of this will be the pronouncing, "Success isn't always determined through using the amount of hours we artwork, however as an opportunity by manner of the impact we make in the moments that really depend."

Introduce Your Topic with a Provocative Quote: Start your presentation with a quote from a famous individual or an authoritative supply this is both concept-scary or motivational. People can also additionally have an emotional response to a quote because of its capacity to connect to them.

Maya Angelou once quoted, "While words might also fade from memory and moves can be neglected, the imprint of approaches you made others revel in remains for all time engraved of their hearts."

Utilize Visual Aids: If the state of affairs requires it, employ visible aids together with props, images, or movies to draw the goal market's attention and make the start of the presentation stand out of their reminiscence.

Visuals have the capability to captivate an goal market and make an effect that remains with them.Displaying an arresting photograph that is applicable on your project depend or playing a quick video clip that prepares the goal marketplace in your presentation or verbal exchange is one instance.

Invoke the Senses: Make an attempt to attraction to the senses of your goal market by way of making use of language this is descriptive and that offers a amazing photograph. Evoke the sensations of the senses in case you need to stimulate the listener's creativeness, emotions, or memories.

Allow your self to have a have a look at the serene symphony of waves colliding inside the direction of the shore, the gentle caress of sand beneath your toes, and the revitalizing fragrance of the ocean breeze as you close your eyes.

Today, we embark on a journey to discover the wonders of coastal conservation."

Establish a Personal Connection: Establish a private reference to your target audience via regarding a previous occasion you each had or an interest you every have in commonplace. This no longer only builds rapport however moreover a experience of familiarity some of the two of you.

Example: "If you've got ever grappled with the disturbing situations of public talking, pass beforehand and raise your hand. Don't fear; you're amongst buddies here. Let's triumph over the ones nerves collectively!" Example: "Raise your hand in case you've ever struggled with public speaking."

Express Your thank you: To begin, it is important to hold your honest thank you or appreciation for the danger to talk in the front of your aim market or to interact with them. Recognize their presence and the contribution they make to the hobby or speak thru manner of thanking them.

Example: "I want to take this opportunity to thank every and every simply absolutely one in all you for being right right here these days. Your presence and participation are the premise of this sizeable communique, and I am truly grateful for the danger to hook up with every and each certainly one of you."

Keep in thoughts that the place to start of your communique want to be tailor-made to the precise environment, target marketplace, and aim of that precise come upon at the way to be attractive. To hone your beginning lines and make sure that they depart a protracted-lasting effect in your listeners, strive out hundreds of strategies, hone your shipping, and be privy to how they are obtained with the aid of the target audience.

Using icebreakers in a whole lot of social settings and conditions

It is important to alter icebreakers regular with the precise social situation wherein they'll be used if you want to assure that they are suitable, relevant, and effective. This is to make sure that they may be utilized efficaciously. It's probably that icebreakers that artwork simply properly in one context won't be as powerful in another surroundings in any respect. The following are a few mind that may be tailored to be used as icebreakers in a huge shape of numerous social settings:

Casual Social Events:

The ice can be broken via the usage of way of asking, "What have become the most memorable tour you have got were given ever taken? When you get together with a set of buddies or pals for a casual gathering, use funny and appealing icebreakers that inspire individuals to proportion their non-public memories. Employing this technique will effectively chip away at any preliminary obstacles, facilitating a continuing transition into an attractive and lively communique. Avoid asking questions that seem overly crucial or expert the least bit charges.

Opportunities for Professional and Personal Networking:

What delivered approximately your preference to return lower back to our event nowadays, and in what enterprise do you presently discover yourself employed?On the concern of events which might be held for the motive of professional networking:

The problem count number "Professional Pathways" is what kicks off the conversation first.

As a thing of the instructions for the occasion, it's miles crucial to encourage people to talk approximately their professional testimonies, interests, and goals in phrases of the hassle recollect of the event or the business enterprise in favored.

Variations:

Elevator Pitch: Instead of asking the human beings a right away query, provide them a described amount of time (for instance, thirty seconds) to introduce themselves and their expert revel in. This gives people with the possibility to rehearse their elevator pitches and create a primary impact so you can stay with them.

Invite individuals to talk approximately a modern expert accomplishment or venture of which they may be especially proud. This can also stimulate conversations concerning people' triumphs, boundaries, and areas of potential.

In order to gather the desires of the collaboration, which is probably to invite human beings to give an cause of their best professional cooperation or partnership, it is able to be beneficial to find out feasible synergies and networking opportunities a number of the members.

Adapting icebreakers for expert networking sports activities at the equal time as keeping a respectful and professional tone can encourage individuals to interact in sizeable conversations, trade contact information, and discover ability collaborations or partnerships. Icebreakers that focus on individuals' professional backgrounds, dreams, and pastimes can facilitate networking and create precious connections in the agency.

Workshops to Construct More Resilient Teams:

Icebreaker: "Unique Connections"

Instructions: Ask every participant to share a humorous or unusual reality approximately themselves that almost all of the people in the group may not understand, and urge them to chose some issue that helps installation relationships or generates dialogues amongst individuals of the crew. The majority of the people in the institution may not understand this records approximately each player.

Variations:

Team Trivia: Instead of sharing person information, divide people into teams and have them wager amusing information approximately every considered one of a kind. Each team can take turns offering their guesses, and the character can each affirm or offer the perfect answer. This encourages collaboration, lively listening, and studying greater approximately teammates.

Picture Perfect: Ask game enthusiasts to deliver a photograph or photo that symbolizes a high-quality trait of themselves. They might also percentage the picture and give an cause in the back of why it is unique to them. This enterprise stimulates visible storytelling and permits people the opportunity to have extra in-intensity conversations.

Lifeline Timeline: Instruct the individuals to acquire a timeline in their lifestyles, which embody non-public and professional milestones. They may also moreover describe key activities and accomplishments, a super manner to foster a sense of shared revel in and information a number of the individuals of the institution.

Icebreakers inclusive of these assist smash down limitations, inspire openness, and gather connections among team members.

They moreover allow members to find out commonalities and appreciate an appropriate features that every crew member brings to the table. The introduction of an surroundings that encourages preserve in thoughts, collaboration, and team bonding is the critical factor to the success of group-building workshops.

Getting Togethers for Companies:

The following is a modified model of the phrase: An icebreaker that celebrates art work-associated accomplishments may assist assemble a pleasant and motivating surroundings in a business organization meeting. It encourages people to talk approximately their victories, that might stimulate others and sell team spirit.

The term "Quarterly Triumphs" is used to interrupt the ice in a communique.

Instructions: Have every player percentage one accomplishment from the maximum state-of-the-art region that they will be specially happy with. This accomplishment will be some thing like a venture that they efficiently finished, a tough goal that they completed, or a milestone that they reached. Encourage them to in brief offer an reason behind why this accomplishment became significant to both themselves or the institution.

Variations:

Team victories: Instead of getting individuals speak about their non-public non-public accomplishments, have them highlight a collective victory that their team or branch executed over the route of the previous region. This allows to construct a experience of cooperation and a apprehend for teamwork.

An amazing icebreaker interest that may help hyperlink the dreams of organization individuals, find out ability regions for help, and set up a enjoy of duty for future successes is to invite people to give an explanation for a expert aim they have got for the subsequent vicinity.

This icebreaker presents an emphasis on appreciation and thankfulness, which permits to foster a healthful manner of existence in the place of business. Create a spherical-robin shape for the "Appreciation Circle," wherein individuals take turns discussing some thing they prefer approximately the character sitting next to them. In this interest, the members take turns discussing a few element they like approximately the person sitting next to them. It offers people of a group with the possibility to have fun each distinct's successes, which enhances morale and motivation inside the corporate surroundings. Additionally, it is able to create a platform for sharing superb practices and training determined out, which contributes to the enterprise's non-stop development and boom. This kind of icebreaker can foster a experience of recognition and validation among coworkers by using specializing in paintings-associated accomplishments and milestones.

Several Varied Examples of Cultural Contexts:

The cookbook titled "Delicious Traditions"

Instructions: Please ask each participant to deliver a dish from their non-public manner of existence or u . S . A . That they do not forget to be one in each of their all-time favorites. Inviting them to in brief provide an explanation for the dish, its significance, and any personal reminiscences or sports activities which might be related to it is a awesome way to get humans talking.

Variations:

Culinary Connections: Instead of that specialize in a single meal, alternatively invite members to speak about a culinary custom or practice this is extremely good to their lifestyle, collectively with a favorite dish or element. This makes it viable for a greater variety of answers and stimulates dialogues about exceptional strategies to the training of food.

This participatory approach allows people to visually connect with meals from lots of cultures and opens the door to possibilities for tasting or the sharing of recipes, provided that the ones sports are practical. Participants in the Cultural Showcase have to take shipping of the choice to bring in each a sample or a picture of the cuisine they've got superb.

Curiosity Regarding Culture Instead of focusing on the cuisine, inspire attendees to speak approximately an thrilling cultural practice, party, or custom from their domestic u . S . A .. Not handiest does this growth the scope of the dialogue, however it moreover encourages people to learn about precise cultural traditions that are not associated with the sector of gastronomy.

When growing icebreakers for situations that embody people from a huge style of cultural backgrounds, it's far critical to hold cultural sensitivities and probably cultural differences in thoughts. Avoid asking questions that could be visible as sensitive, insulting, or limited to nice faiths or cultures. The contributors may be capable to speak about and respect their cultural origins in a way this is each extraordinary and attractive if an environment that is courteous and inclusive is created.

Activities Relating to Learning or the Academic Profession:

These varieties of icebreakers are an awesome manner to get human beings speakme approximately widespread topics and to set the tone for an intellectually stimulating surroundings. The modified model is as follows:

The phrase "Recent Academic Discoveries" is a planned try and ease people into the verbal exchange.

Instructions: Ask every person to talk approximately a piece of captivating records or a discovery that they made these days due to their intellectual pastimes or studies. This might be some thing from a latest fact to some component that they uncovered, and also you must inspire them to provide a succinct justification for why they find this precise piece of statistics to be charming.

Variations:

test Revelations: Instead of speaking about favored information, have the contributors communicate approximately a modern have a look at discovery or article that they've right here across. This makes it possible to have more in-depth conversations approximately educational interests and viable chances for collaborative artwork.

You may be capable of get people extra invested within the communication if, in place of asking them to provide records, you ask them to speak approximately an educational goal they intend to gather or a studies venture they are passionate about. This allows people to unique their educational pastimes and may result in individuals discovering hobbies they have got in commonplace with each other.

Ask the people to talk approximately their views and take part in civilized communicate. This encourages analytical wondering similarly to intellectually stimulating conversations within the classroom. Critical debates require the presentation of a notion-provoking issue or contentious situation be counted this is linked to the occasion's problem don't forget.

It is crucial, on the identical time as adapting icebreakers for academic contexts, to consider the individual of the event in addition to the educational backgrounds of the participants. The surrender end result of this venture need to be the appearance of an surroundings that encourages highbrow hobby, instructional advancement, and significant connections amongst humans. These icebreakers have the capability to function the starting point for attractive instructional conversations and the improvement of individuals of the own family.

A chat that is aimed to interrupt the ice could possibly flow into a few thing like this: "Find a person you have never met earlier than and percentage one problem you're looking ahead to at this event."

Adaptation: At massive gatherings, make use of activities that inspire internet web page site visitors to network with one another and hook up with each other. Choose sports activities that help wreck the ice for absolutely everyone who may be tense by way of manner of the big variety of folks who are in attendance Activities that inspire guests to network with each other and hook up with each distinctive.

Get-Togethers for Socializing on a Smaller, More Personal Scale:

When preserving sports which might be small and personal, it is important to pick out icebreakers that inspire participants to move further into speak and offer them the possibility to connect on a greater private diploma. These icebreakers assemble huge encounters via developing a experience of openness and vulnerability amongst folks that take part. The changed model of this sentence is as follows:

A place to begin for a dialogue utilising the word "Passionate Pursuits"

Instruct each participant that you need them to speak about a interest or interest that they have been devoting more hobby to these days, and inspire them to talk about the motives why they may be so obsessed on it, in addition to any private reviews or successes which are connected to their selected project.

Variations:

Show-and-Tell with a Creative Spin Encourage participants to hold a photo or object that exemplifies what they do in area of truly speakme about their interests or pastimes. This will offer a innovative spin on the interest. Participants can be in a function to expose it to others and speak its relevance, which can also cause extra in-intensity dialogues and interactions.

Participants need to be requested to offer an reason behind the history in their preferred interest or hobby in the segment that is labeled "Personal Journeys." Encourage them to tell about how they stumbled onto it, what attracted them to it, and the manner their lives have changed due to their involvement with it. This paves the manner for people to percent private recollections and reports with each different.Invite the alternative individuals of the agency to determine if there are any similarities or links most of the player's interests and their own. This have to lead to conversations approximately potential partnerships or activities that each parties can take part in collectively. Collaborative links: After all and sundry has shared their interest or interest, invite the possibility people of the company to decide if there are any similarities or links some of the player's pastimes and their personal.

These icebreakers allow individuals to percentage their interests, reminiscences, and personal trips with the company so that you can assemble a experience of statistics and empathy maximum of the human beings of the organization. The purpose of enhancing icebreakers for use at small and intimate sports is to create an environment that is constant and comfortable, thereby permitting people to have interaction with every different on a deeper diploma.

Situations that could arise on-line or in a virtual surroundings are numerous. Here are a few examples:

It is critical to alter icebreakers for scenarios in which they will take place digitally as a way to make sure that participants will maintain their interest inside the hobby and connect with one another. The following is the adjustment that modified into made to be used in digital environments:

Icebreaker: "Digital Discoveries"

Instructions: Ask each participant to make contributions one captivating fact approximately the virtual global that they have determined out in the previous 3 hundred and sixty 5 days. It may be some issue present day, which incorporates a bit of era, a modern-day day virtual style, a internet web site, or maybe an revel in linked to a few form of digital occasion. Encourage them to offer a succinct clarification of why they discover it captivating or the manner it has prompted them every for my part or professionally.

Variations:

Virtual Adventures: Instead of concentrating at the virtual international in stylish, ask individuals to share an uncommon or particular enjoy they have got had with virtual occasions, webinars, or on line collaborations. This may be completed through asking individuals to inform a story approximately a time once they participated in a digital occasion. This may also additionally moreover bring up conversations on the demanding situations of virtual engagement further to progressive solutions to those annoying situations.

Recommendations Regarding Technology As an opportunity to discussing some thing that they've located, contributors may be requested to indicate a beneficial digital tool, utility, or net internet site that they have got encounter and positioned to be valuable. This model encourages members to percentage their understanding with one another and may furthermore expose them to new property.

Chapter 3: Non-Verbal Communication

Small communicate is based carefully on non-verbal communique because it allows for the expression of feelings, attitudes, and intentions even inside the absence of vocal trade. During informal conversation, a few vital characteristics of nonverbal conversation to keep in mind embody the subsequent:

Make Eye Contact

During small chat, it's far vital to make and preserve adequate eye touch. This demonstrates which you are actively listening and worried inside the topic. It allows set up a connection between the two of you on the identical time as moreover demonstrating that you are inquisitive about what the possibility individual is saying. Having stated that, it's far important to find out a glad medium. Avoiding eye touch may possibly deliver the have an effect on which you are uninterested or unconcerned, while making excessive use of eye contact may be intense or scary. Strive for eye touch that is simple and comfortable, and appearance far from the man or woman every so often to keep away from staring.

Facial Expressions:

Because they're able to constitute this type of big sort of emotions, facial expressions are robust system that can be finished in small chat. Smiling is one of the simplest strategies to result in an environment this is warmness and inviting. It demonstrates which you are type and inquisitive about the speak that is occurring. However, because it is easy to choose out up on fake or pressured grins, you have to make sure that your expressions are right. Make certain that your facial expressions correspond to the tenor of the speak and that they transmit the relevant feelings.

Gestures:

When challenge small speak, the use of hand movements and gestures can assist to make clear and improve the which means of what you are saying. You can use them to deliver a tale, display your passion, or spotlight crucial factors for your argument. However, hold in mind the propriety of your gestures further to the cultural norms associated with them. It's vital to persuade smooth of incredibly forceful or immoderate motions that might likely detract from or dominate the discourse.

Posture:

It is critical to hold up a wholesome posture even if undertaking casual verbal exchange. Maintaining an upright posture, whether or now not status or seated, communicates alertness and self perception. It demonstrates both that you are respectful of the alternative individual and which you are actively worried within the discourse. On the opportunity hand, adopting an thoughts-set that offers off the appearance which you are closed off or bored stiff can be finished through using manner of crossing your arms and legs. It is critical to be privy to your posture in case you need to offer a pleasing and open individual.

Proximity:

Because the concept of personal location differs from way of life to life-style, it's far important to take heed to the right degree of proximity while sporting out small chat. In favored, displaying respect for the alternative individual's private region consists of maintaining a distance that is comfortable for them. They may also feel uneasy if you stand too near them, but in case you stand too a ways away, you may probable deliver them the effect that you don't care about them. Adjust yourself to the events and the cues given through the opposite individual as a manner to find out the most suitable distance physical.

Mirroring:

During small chat, subtly imitating the frame language of the other individual can assist generate a revel in of connection and rapport some of the two of you. This approach consists of replicating the intention man or woman's gestures, body posture, or perhaps tone of voice to a few diploma. It contributes to the development of a sense of familiarity and demonstrates that you are sensitive to the manner in which they talk. However, mirroring need to be executed in a natural manner and must no longer be completed excessively. This is as it need to flow with the speak and have to not come off as mimicking.

Nodding in agreement whilst listening:

During small speak, it's miles viable to demonstrate active listening the usage of non-verbal signs and symptoms together with nodding. When a person is speaking to you, it's far polite to nod your head occasionally to signify which you are paying interest and which you recognize what they may be pronouncing. It demonstrates that you fee their input even as moreover encouraging them to preserve sharing what they apprehend. Nodding, at the aspect of maintaining eye contact, is a brilliant manner to reveal which you are engaged within the communication being had.

The tenor of one's voice

When assignment small chat, the way in which you speak, specially your tone of voice, is critical. A horrible have an effect on may be made even though the challenge rely of your comments is upbeat, especially in case your tone is antagonistic or repetitive. Aim for a type and inviting tone this is constant with the vibe of the communication you are having. A tone this is tremendous permits to installation a setting that is comfortable and attractive, and it may furthermore beneficial resource to the approach of building rapport with the opportunity character.

Pacing:

When carrying out small chat, it's far critical to be aware of how fast or slowly the communication is moving. Give the alternative character the possibility to talk with out being interrupted, and try now not to talk too speedy for the scenario. If you pass too short via the communique, the possibility person may additionally revel in as even though they'll be no longer being heard or as despite the fact that their opinion does no longer rely. Maintain attention of the development of the conversation and search for possibilities to invite participation from the opposite individual via inviting them to offer their thoughts and reviews.

Feel (and use the proper tenses):

During polite verbal exchange, a few mild touches can be appropriate in superb cultural settings and social conditions. Warmth and connection may be communicated by means of way of the use of bodily touch, which include a handshake or a slap at the decrease decrease back. Having stated that, it's miles crucial to honor one's private limitations in addition to the standards of 1's manner of existence. Take care now not to initiate touch till you're high-quality that it's far going to be welcomed genuinely, or maybe then, hold with warning. When uncertain, it's miles fine to avoid making bodily contact with the alternative character and as an alternative recognition on exclusive strategies of non-verbal communication.

Keep in mind that the nuanced and context-hooked up nature of non-verbal communication is an vital element of small chat. Enhancing the first-rate of your interactions can be finished with the useful resource of first being aware about your personal non-verbal cues after which paying near hobby to the cues given off with the beneficial useful resource of the other person. Adjust your non-verbal communique so you can foster an environment this is welcoming and upbeat, one which encourages actual involvement and connection even as you are doing small communication.

Acquiring an consciousness of the affect that frame language and facial feelings will have.

There is a thriller language that exists within the expansive problem of verbal exchange, and it regularly consists of greater weight than words by myself. The language of frame language and facial expressions—the silent messengers that display a universe of feelings, intentions, and connections—is the language in question. Learning to decipher the that means on the returned of those nonverbal signs and symptoms is need to cracking a code that unlocks the door to charming communication. Therefore, allow us to exit on an adventure to find out their secrets and techniques and techniques and techniques and discover ways to harness their electricity.

Imagine a scenario wherein our ability to speak is impaired and our feelings well up inner us like a flood. In those occasions, it's far the involuntary twitch of a grin or the subtle furrowing of the brow that betrays our right feelings. Our faces, which are like canvases, disclose the elaborate sun shades of our souls, growing colorful snap shots of feelings which consist of happiness, disappointment, surprise, and fury. In the dance of body language, every gesture will become a brushstroke, weaving a story of self-guarantee, warm temperature, or distance, counting on how the gesture is completed.

The rhythm of our presence is determined by way of manner of our posture, which then creates a massive symphony. A tall, erect stance communicates a experience of self-guarantee and invitations others to concentrate, at the same time as extended fingers provide connection and show a willingness to be inclined. Every motion and gesture we make accentuates what we're announcing, affords emphasis while crucial, and draws hobby to what we have to mention like a magnet.And lest we neglect, the eyes are the portals via which the soul communicates with the frame. They do not want to utter a single word to maintain a first rate deal of which means that. Through them, we're capable of shape connections, which in turn pave the way for extra comprehension and empathy. We can transmit encouragement, hobby, or maybe a mild venture with surely the advent that we deliver someone. The volume of one's eye contact is similar to an unseen thread that knits consider and intimacy, so important dialogues to hitherto unexplored degrees of profundity.

Microexpressions are like ephemeral brushstrokes which can be painted on the canvas that is our faces all through this symphony of non-verbal communique. A transient glimpse of happiness, a muffled flash of astonishment, or the wrinkled lines of tension can all be visible within the ones split-2nd home windows in which the fact can be seen to emerge. These microexpressions, which can be similar to hushed revelations, inspire us to analyze similarly, skip at the back of the floor, and unearth the recollections which might be concealed there.

But permit us to not permit the lenses of our personal lifestyle to restrict our wondering. Body language and facial emotions dance to their personal top notch rhythms throughout a extensive form of cultural contexts. The expression of astonishment in one subculture can be visible as skepticism in every unique manner of existence while the eyebrow is lifted. When we're sensitive to and privy to the intricacies of a situation, we are higher prepared to bridge cultural divides and domesticate right connections that bypass beyond borders.

Embrace this thriller language, as it has the potential to win people's hearts and minds. Mastering the symphony of your body language and the poetry of your facial feelings is an brilliant manner to increase yourself-awareness. Allow them to create a fascinating ensemble at the side of your words thru harmonizing with them. This will purpose it to resonate with the people round you.

In the charming vicinity of communication, in which phrases can most effective skim the floor, you could create a masterpiece collectively with your frame language and facial expressions. Unlock the mysteries they disguise, tap into the power they very own, and spark off on a journey wherein every stumble upon transforms into an entrancing dance of connecting with and comprehending the alternative individuals.

As we discover greater into the charming worldwide of non-verbal communication, we discover that it possesses an first-rate capacity to have an impact on and mold the relationships we've got got with every other. We have the power, similar to that of finished magicians, to captivate an purpose marketplace with our frame language and facial feelings and to head away an impact this is hard to forget about.

Imagine having a conversation wherein your terms go with the flow like water via the air, but it's miles your body language that creates a hypnotic spell for the opposite character. You are capable of rapidly captivate hobby and convey others into your magnetic presence really through way of keeping an confident posture and flashing a type smile. The moderate tilt of your head communicates which you are actively listening, which encourages the person who is talking to express their critiques and tales with actual enthusiasm.

In this hypnotic dance, gestures take on the function of the conductor's baton, and they're liable for directing the communicative symphony. Your planned hand motions assist to heighten crucial thoughts and generate colourful pics in the minds of your target market on the equal time as you talk. Your frame language exudes ardour, conviction, and authenticity, elevating smooth phrases into riveting performances that emotionally reverberate with the purpose market.

And then there are your eyes, which might be like home windows that draw people in and mirror the fireside that burns inner you. They shine with an eagerness to investigate, losing mild on the topic available on the identical time as additionally encouraging others to make contributions their elements of view. You should make a huge reference to someone certainly through searching into their eyes and so create a regular environment wherein mind and feelings are loose to waft. The expression for your eyes conveys comprehension, empathy, and a sincere hobby in the tales which is probably gambling out within the the front of you.

Microexpressions are the brilliant fireworks that stimulate fascination and curiosity on this entrancing tapestry, this is why it is so compelling. You offer the affect which you have a hidden stage of comprehension with only a brief raising of an eyebrow or a quick sparkle in every eye. Others get curious and lean in nearer, as notwithstanding the truth that they're enthralled thru the name of the sport and geared up to decipher the numerous layers of your thoughts and feelings.

Your recognition of non-verbal cues turns into your compass as you flow into through a number of social conditions and civilizations. In order to expose recognize for cultural norms and sensitivity, you alter each your body language and the expressions for your face. Because of your adaptability and open-mindedness, you are able to near gaps, domesticate connections, and create stories which might be so enticing that they move beyond boundaries.

Nevertheless, allow us to now not forget approximately the reality that the authenticity of this entrancing dance is the most critical factor. When your body language and facial emotions in form with who you virtually are, they turn out to be signs of a real connection among you and the opposite person. People are drawn to your honesty, and they find out every solace and thought inside the fact which you emanate realness in your interactions with them.

Therefore, allow us to start on this experience of captivating non-verbal conversation, in which each movement, each expression, and each stare produces a vibrant masterpiece. You can also moreover seize humans's hearts, minds, and souls with the useful resource of gaining knowledge of the energy of your body language and the expressions for your face. Embrace this bold electricity bestowed upon you and harness it to your benefit. Let the arena be your degree, and might your non-verbal symphony make an eternal impact at the minds of everybody who are lucky sufficient to have the possibility to have a have a study it.

Chapter 4: Maintaining Suitable Eye Touch

During small speak, its miles important to keep suitable eye touch, gestures, and posture so as to engage in effective speak and make a fine first have an effect on. In order to address those issues effectively even as task small chat, right right right here are some suggestions:

Eye touch:

Maintain suitable eye touch through looking proper away into the eyes of the character you are talking with; however, keep away from staring deeply into their eyes for the reason that this can motive them to revel in uneasy. On the opportunity side, fending off eye contact may additionally additionally create the impact that you are fed up inside the problem remember handy or which you lack self guarantee.

Act in a way that is easy and unforced. Make an try to appear herbal and unaffected whilst you're starting eye contact. Relax the muscles for your face and allow your gaze to move freely most of the hassle's eyes and the relaxation of their face at the equal time as you take a look at them. If you want to keep away from conveying tension or ache, you have to avoid searching fixedly or darting your eyes spherical an excessive quantity. In order to make certain complete coverage, it's miles important to take the subsequent factors into hobby as well:

Make eye touch to communicate your degree of hobby. Maintaining eye contact sends a message to the possibility person that you are actively involved inside the conversation and interested in what they have got to mention by using manner of permitting them to understand which you are listening to what they're announcing. It demonstrates appreciate and attentiveness, which lets in to cultivate a bond most of the two of you.

Consider how lengthy you need to make eye contact for: the time frame you have to spend doing so can exchange relying on cultural conventions and person comfort levels. In most situations, making and retaining eye contact for intervals of three to 5 seconds at a time is deemed suitable. To prevent the alternative individual from feeling overpowered or tested, however, it's far vital to consider to sometimes damage eye contact with them.

Adjust your eye contact in step with the context, as precise social activities can also moreover demand for special tiers of that interaction. When having a communique with just a different individual, instead of in a bigger institution setting, retaining eye contact is of intense importance. Eye contact need to be shared some of the various members in a discourse taking vicinity in a set putting for you to ensure that everybody feels included.

Recognize and honor the boundaries of others. Although maintaining eye contact is vital, it's also critical to be respectful of personal space and the consolation zones of others. It's viable that a few human beings's cultural backgrounds or private alternatives make it tough for them to make direct eye contact. If you take a look at every other man or woman keeping off eye contact, it's miles simply beneficial to apprehend their boundaries and no longer try to maintain eye contact with them for an extended time body.

Keep in thoughts that preserving eye touch is nice one part of having a fulfillment conversations. It contributes to the introduction of a amazing and thrilling enjoy in small verbal exchange, specially while blended with attentive listening, proper frame language, and proper hobby. Managing eye touch at the identical time as having discussions turns into masses less hard and extra herbal for you in case you positioned those competencies into exercising in a number of various social context.

Make sure to interrupt eye contact sometimes: If you do no longer want the conversation to feel too immoderate, ensure to interrupt eye contact now and again through glancing away for a 2d or looking extremely good spots on their face.

Gestures:

Be herbal: Make use of motions which may be familiar to you and that correctly portray your character. It is crucial to avoid acting dishonest or distracting others with the resource of going overboard or utilizing actions which is probably overly dramatic.

Your hand movements and body language have to reward what you're saying, reinforcing your thoughts or adding importance to your expressions. This can be completed via matching your gestures in conjunction with your phrases. The following is a few in addition data:

Be cognizant of cultural versions. In a few cultures, some hand gestures are herbal and time-commemorated however in others, the identical gestures can be seen as insulting or incorrect. It is crucial to be aware of these variations and modify your gestures correctly whilst taking element in small speak with people from numerous cultural backgrounds. Spend some time reading the community customs and traditions on the way to prevent any awkwardness or confusion which can rise up.

Use movements to demonstrate your arguments. Use hand moves to visually illustrate what you are saying whilst you're telling a story or explaining some thing in some unspecified time in the future of small verbal exchange. For instance, in case you're telling a story or explaining a few issue. For example, in case you are describing a massive fish which you caught whilst fishing, you may display the dimensions of the fish thru preserving up your fingers. This offers depth on your story and makes it less complex for the listener to understand the factor you are trying to make.

Make nice that your motions are in tune with the tone of your voice. Your facial expressions, your tone of voice, and the sensation which you deliver to your words need to all be congruent with each other. For example, in case you're speaking about an thrilling difficulty be counted, you need to make your gestures greater lively and enthusiastic. When you are speakme approximately something that is solemn or horrifying, instead, your frame language want to mirror a extra muted tone.

Try to keep away from making any motions that look uneasy or repeated. It is essential to be aware about any repetitive gestures you may be making, in conjunction with tapping your hands or fidgeting, as those may be distracting and are signs and symptoms of anxiety. Instead, located your attention on gestures which have a motive and lend each meaning and importance to what you're pronouncing.

Pay near interest to the gestures that the opportunity individual is making. Be conscious of the possibility character's frame language as you communicate with them through gesturing yourself and listening to how they gesture. Their posture, facial expressions, and gestures can all provide insightful clues about their feelings and stage of participation. If you've got a examine that they'll be using amazing gestures, it could be a signal that they will be interested by a specific problem or that they may be placing cognizance on a selected problem.

Exercise each by way of manner of yourself within the front of a mirror or collectively together with your friends. If you are unsure of your gestures, you ought to rehearse in the front of a reflect or ask a chum for remarks and then make any important adjustments. When you have interaction in small communicate, turning into familiar collectively with your natural motions will make you appear greater self-confident and right to others round you.

It is critical to hold in mind that the purpose of making use of gestures on the identical time as mission small communicate is to beautify the super of the dialogue and to inspire a effective connection with the opposite individual. You may additionally additionally make your communication extra engaging and exceptional with the useful aid of using gestures which might be herbal for you, that come from the coronary heart, and which is probably supportive of what you are saying.

Posture:

Maintain an upright stance or posture. A confident and alert look can be conveyed through properly posture. Slouching can deliver the have an effect on which you are fed up or unapproachable, so try to keep away from doing it.

Take care not to invade the gap of others. Stand or sit down at a suitable distance from the alternative character to show which you respect their right to private location. It is feasible that you may make them experience uneasy if you invade their private place.

Be sincere on your smile:

When assignment small talk, smiling allows create an environment that is friendlier and extra approachable. A actual grin has the electricity to every placed a few different character cushty and inspire them to have a positive communication.

Subtly reflect the other person's frame language:

Establishing rapport with a few different character and growing a feel of connection may be aided with the aid of subtly mirroring the possibility person's body language. Be cautious not to be too obvious to your imitating their gestures, as this may be interpreted as cheating or as an try and make amusing of them.

Be attentive:

Pay interest to the nonverbal signs and symptoms that the other individual is providing you with as nicely. This will can help you determine whether or not or not they're interested by the communication, permitting you to regulate your gestures and posture efficiently.

Maintain an energetic listening exercise:

The art work of making small talk consists of more than truely talking; it additionally calls for attentive listening. Demonstrate that you are listening to what the opportunity character is pronouncing through manner of nodding on occasion and efficaciously replying to what they may be announcing.

It is essential to keep in thoughts that the name of the game to creating exquisite small speak is to strike a balance among paying interest and engaged at the same time as additionally respecting the limits and comfort levels of the other character. Maintain a sincere and honest demeanor in all of your encounters, and artwork on honing those capabilities on a normal basis to frequently enhance your verbal exchange abilties.

Chapter 5: Small Talk In Specific Contexts

Making the transition from idle chitchat to sizable exchanges

A knowledge that is vital for developing deeper connections and forming relationships which can be extra excellent with precise human beings is the ability to move from small communicate to conversations that are large. The following are some strategies with a purpose to help you in making that adjustment:

Find out whether or not or no longer or now not you have got got any pursuits, passions, or reports in common with this character so you can experience doing subjects collectively. You can create a herbal get proper of entry to element for deeper conversations by manner of manner of searching out matters which you have in commonplace with the opportunity man or woman. For example, in case you find out that you and each other individual percentage a passion for hiking, you can begin a communique about your preferred hikes, the maximum memorable reports you have got got had, or the connection amongst spending time in nature and personal development.

Ask open-ended questions. Asking the opportunity character open-ended questions compels them to offer responses which are each more in-intensity and similarly reflective. Instead of asking honest positive-or-no questions, interest your inquiry on the person's perspectives, values, or research. This lets in the controversy to progress and opens the door to greater in-intensity studies. For example, in location of asking in the event that they determine upon films, you could inquire approximately their desired movie and the reasons why it struck a chord with them.

Demonstrate a honest hobby: In order to successfully transition into tremendous talks, it's far vital to illustrate a honest hobby in the ideas and testimonies of the possibility person. Follow-up questions are a extraordinary manner to reveal off your hobby and display which you are curious. This demonstrates that you appreciate their point of view and are sincerely inquisitive about gaining a deeper understanding of them.

Share your non-public research: When people percent their non-public personal stories and critiques with each different, it is able to generate a experience of vulnerability and consider, which in turn encourages the possibility man or woman to open up. Maintain honesty and provide pertinent anecdotes or reflections which might be germane to the hassle being mentioned. When you communicate about the topics that have befell to you to your existence, it may bring about greater in-intensity talks and bring together a higher connection among you and the opportunity person.

It is critical to have interaction in energetic listening. To have interaction in lively listening, one need to concentrate one's whole interest at the alternative character which will virtually realize what they're announcing. You must refrain from interrupting them and provide them your entire interest as an alternative. Maintain eye touch with the individual you're paying attention to, nod every now and then, and use vocal clues to demonstrate that you understand and are interested in what's being stated. It is crucial to indicate that you have in reality listened to the other man or woman and comprehended their mind-set through reflecting again on what they have said.

Be empathic: To show empathy, you should make a concerted effort to understand the emotions, testimonies, and factors of view of the alternative man or woman. Validate their emotions and show that you can apprehend topics from their mindset via responding as it should be. Avoid passing judgment or disregarding their mind, and as an alternative work to installation a welcoming surroundings wherein they will be cushty being open approximately how they experience and what they have got to mention.

Ask deeper inquiries about feelings. Explore the extra emotive facets of the issues which can be currently being spoken about to inspire extra in-depth conversations. You can also have deeper and more extremely good conversations with people if you ask them approximately their emotions and the effect that precise activities had on them. If you're speakme to a person approximately their cutting-edge merchandising, as an instance, you need to inquire about how they felt once they located out the information and what it method to them on a personal stage.

Avoid debatable problems till appropriate. It is important to pick out the appropriateness of the event further to the extent of comfort of the character you are speakme with. Even even though enormous talks can also embody speakme about extra weighty or controversial topics, it's miles vital to carry out that. If you have had been given any inkling that the challenge available might be sensitive or divisive, you want to method it with excessive warning or shift the focus of the verbal exchange to some thing else that both activities will have interaction with in a comfortable manner.

Be affected character and non-judgmental. Patience and an open thoughts are prerequisites for having significant interactions. Let the alternative character stop their idea with out being rushed or interrupted, and pay attention to what they have got to say. Maintain a nonjudgmental mind-set and get keep of various humans's thoughts, thoughts, and factors of view, despite the truth that they vary from your very non-public. This establishes an environment of agree with and openness, which promotes discussions to enter more intensity.

Create a regular area. Create a setting that is both steady and scary for the alternative individual to be able to sense snug expressing their thoughts and emotions. Be aware about your replies, in addition to your body language and tone of voice, to ensure that you are cultivating an environment that is accepting and understanding of others. Create an surroundings wherein neither celebration feels threatened or judged, and in which they will freely communicate their mind and emotions with every unique.

Through the implementation of these strategies, you may be able to rework meaningless chatter into applicable and thrilling conversations. Keep in thoughts that cultivating massive relationships takes time and effort, and that you could sell more tremendous encounters with human beings through actively contributing and demonstrating real hobby inner the problem depend handy.

Conversations with numerous clients: A high-quality part of providing superior customer support is interacting with customers in a pleasant and conversational manner. It contributes to the appearance of a heat and inviting surroundings, enables to installation a non-public connection, and improves the complete enjoy that a purchaser has. Here are a few pointers that could assist you have interaction in small communication with customers extra correctly:

Beginning the communique with a pleasant and sincere hiya is a exceptional way to set the tone for the rest of it. A sincere "Hello" or "Welcome" establishes a nice tone and informs the consumer which you are organized to provide help to them.

Find some factor you've got were given in common with the alternative man or woman with the resource of seeking out shared reviews or pastimes that can be used as a springboard for verbal exchange. This ought to check with something from modern happenings to well-known landmarks within the place, or perhaps the goods or services which you offer. Developing a reference to a person via the invention of some issue they have in not unusual with you enables to make the communication greater interesting.

In order to inspire clients to offer extra statistics about themselves, it's miles useful to pose questions which might be open-ended. It demonstrates that you are interested by their thoughts and viewpoints at the equal time as you try this. You may additionally, as an instance, inquire about their plans for the approaching weekend or their skip-to item from the aforementioned reputation quo.

Active listening includes listening to what the customer is saying and demonstrating actual interest in what they have to mention. Keep eye touch, nod your head, and offer verbal cues to demonstrate which you are paying hobby and actively listening. This not best famous respect for the client however furthermore makes them experience valued.

The communicate need to be personalised: Whenever it is viable, the chat want to be custom designed via utilising the client's call or addressing any beyond encounters you may have had with them. This no longer simplest demonstrates that you don't forget the man or woman, however it furthermore makes the occasion feel more customized.

Maintain a contented and upbeat thoughts-set. Maintain a pleasant mind-set and steer clear of delving into contentious or touchy topics. Put your hobby on topics which might be exciting to customers and characteristic the capability to enhance their disposition. This contributes to the overall pleasantness of the stumble upon and ultimately leaves the purchaser with an excellent impact.

Give them your entire interest. Always preserve the patron's time and the state of affairs in which you are interacting in thoughts. If they may be in a rush or look preoccupied, hold the small communique short and targeted on their straight away desires. This will display attention for his or her state of affairs. In the occasion that they are extra relaxed or inclined to have interaction in talk, you could regulate the quantity of small speak ultimately.

Use small chat as a device to advantage insights: Using small communicate as a device to build up insights can offer valuable facts into the options, desires, or remarks of the consumer. Pay hobby to the facts that customers offer with you for the duration of more casual chats, as this can help you adapt your provider or discover possibilities to beautify the consumer enjoy.

Pay hobby to the purchaser's frame language and one-of-a-type non-verbal clues. This is an essential difficulty of imparting exquisite customer support. Respect their barriers and put your interest on giving issuer this is every powerful and attentive even though they appear bored stiff or reticent. Make changes on your method in keeping with how snug they are.

Follow up with the patron displaying which you are in truth interested by what they have got to mention: If it's far suitable, have a look at up on in advance conversations or interactions the client has had with you. This demonstrates which you remember them similarly to which you care about the enjoy they had. You also can, as an instance, inquire about their maximum modern buy or inquire approximately their enjoy with a particular item.

Keep in thoughts that any small talk you have with a customer want to usually be geared in the path of the patron, need to be respectful, and ought to are in search of to make their revel in higher. You may additionally moreover forge deeper connections with people and make an effect which will remaining if you domesticate an environment that is upbeat and exciting.

Chapter 6: Small Conversations For Introverts

Introverts, who may additionally experience extra comfortable with deeper, more vital talks, might also moreover discover it hard to have interaction in small speak at times. Despite this, making small speak remains a crucial social capabilities for introverts to collect because it facilitates them hook up with others and form relationships. Here are a few strategies for introverts to barter small talk:

Take some time to get prepared in advance than going to any social activities or interactions wherein small talk is expected, and you will be an lousy lot greater snug. Consider some possible topics or questions that you could convey up in one among a type forms of interactions. When it involves making small communication, having finished some training ahead can assist ease a number of the anxiousness and create a enjoy of self-assure.

Pick the notable configuration to your wishes. Discover settings or sports that are congruent with the property you are enthusiastic about. It is a wonderful deal easier to take part in conversations while you are in an environment that feels natural and snug to you. Search for chances wherein you can connect to others over shared hobbies, along with interest companies, ebook golf equipment, or expert networking sports activities, and take advantage of those after they present themselves.

Actively pay attention: Introverts have a recognition for being suitable listeners, that is a feature that can be leveraged all through small chat. Concentrate on in truth listening to the opportunity individual in place of stressful approximately whether or no longer or not you need to be the only to guide the communique. In order to illustrate which you are genuinely inquisitive about what they're pronouncing, you need to ask comply with-up questions. You also can make a superb have an impact on on others and build rapport with them thru listening cautiously and being attentive to what they have got to say.

Find a thing of settlement. Try to discover a few commonplace ground, inclusive of pursuits or reviews, to use as a springboard for verbal exchange. These subjects that we've got in common can feature a bridge among superficial small communicate and deeper, more meaningful interactions. For instance, in case you and the alternative character find out which you have a interest in common, you might be able to bypass deeper into the concern matter and percentage your stories with each other.

When it is critical, take breaks. People who are greater introverted typically refuel themselves via spending time alone. Give your self permission to take breaks whenever you enjoy the want to while you are taking part in social sports that incorporate small conversation. Find a while to step away, supply yourself a chance to entice your breath, and refuel your energies. You might not turn out to be as socially worn out if you do this as it will assist you hold your experience of equilibrium.

Instead than feeling compelled to interact in a big quantity of discussions along side insignificant small chat, interest on the exquisite of the interactions in desire to the amount of talks you have. Have fewer discussions ordinary, but make sure every one counts. Taking this approach permits you to channel your power into growing deeper relationships with one of a kind human beings.

Accept and embody who you truly are. When mission small speak, you should not revel in the need to region on an act of extrovertism. Accept the truth that you are an introvert and be dependable to who you're. People like authenticity, and in case you display off authenticity, you can lure others who fee you for who you are and recognize you for that.

When taking part in small conversations, it's far important to ask open-ended questions because they stimulate extra in-intensity responses. These are the sorts of inquiries that name for additonal than a honest "yes" or "no" reaction and open the door to a higher talk. Queries on the side of "What are your mind on..." and "Can you tell me more about..." are both examples of open-ended queries.

Seek out one-on-one discussions: Introverts may additionally moreover discover that one-on-one talks are plenty much less complicated to deal with and much more likely to result in substantial exchanges within the occasion that they searching for them out. If in any respect feasible, you want to search for possibilities to have more non-public, closed-door conversations with fewer humans so that you might also moreover additionally have extra in-intensity exchanges.

Chapter 7: The Influence Of Better Small Talk

Small chat may additionally seem little, however it possesses a strong strain this is going beyond the superficial. It is the spark that ignites long-lasting friendships, the catalyst for expert probabilities, and the glue that holds groups collectively. We ought to first recognize the intricacies of powerful small verbal exchange to be able to harness this capability.

1.1 Networking Events: The Dreadful Obstacle

Networking gatherings, with their call tags and awkward mingling, frequently instill worry and tension. We've all been there: seeking to strike up significant discussions whilst secretly wishing we may be some other place. But what if we recommended you that the ones sports do not need to be feared? You can remodel networking meetings into opportunities to shine if you have the proper small chat skills.

Imagine getting into a room whole of strangers and with a chunk of success placing up great conversations. No more awkward silences or anxiety—as an alternative, you may be the individual others are looking for out, eager to engage with. In this ebook, we can offer you the device you need to overcome those social disturbing conditions, transforming networking activities into opportunities to be successful.

1.2 The Value of Informal Conversation

Small chat is more than clearly a social lubricant; it's far the foundation for extra significant interactions. It's the stepping stone that allows you to interact in more in-depth, large talks. Small chat can also moreover flip strangers into pals, colleagues into collaborators, and strangers into allies.

In a world at the same time as first impressions are everything, reading the art work of small communication can open formerly closed doors. Understanding the importance of a success small conversation is the first step in the direction of sporting out your dreams, whether or not or now not they be personal boom, career success, or enriching relationships.

1.Three Your Path to Becoming a Small Talk Expert

Are you prepared to move on a self-improvement and social reform journey? This e book is your street map to turning into a draw close of small chat. We'll stroll you via the approach of mastering small talk little by little, no matter what your gift diploma of social self belief is.

We draw on plenty of sources, starting from clinical research to real-life opinions, to offer you with sensible, actionable guidance. Patrick King, popular author and social abilties educate, has condensed years of experience into one thorough manual. He is acquainted with the problems of social touch for my part, having been a shy introvert himself. He's now here to percent his information and knowledge with you.

You can discover the following data on the following pages:

How to strike up a communique with a stranger and begin a speak with self belief.

Techniques for averting awkward silences and maintaining talks on foot smoothly.

Strategies for pushing beyond ground-diploma chitchat and into big discussions.

Conversational techniques that function the least bit ranges of the communique, from greeting to good-bye.

How to inform exciting memories and make your anecdotes unforgettable.

Techniques for developing a welcoming and open surroundings that locations others relaxed.

The commonplace conversational styles you need to damage, further to the tiny adjustments that would make a huge difference.

By the stop of "Better Small Talk," you will have a toolbox complete of precise dialogues, responses, phrases, and questions to apply in lots of scenarios. You'll broaden a magnetic character that outcomes attracts new pals and connections.

Remember that simple speak opens the door to friendships, expert success, romantic relationships, and fashionable delight. The capability to connect to absolutely everyone is an underappreciated superpower. People is probably interested in you for no obvious purpose, and you may by no means once more bore them in some unspecified time in the future of chats.

So, if you're geared up to make each communique rely, if you're equipped to understand small speak, turn the internet page and permit the adventure begin. Unlock the strength of Better Small Talk with the useful resource of clicking the BUY NOW button at the top of the web web page.

Chapter 8: The Ice The Art Of Making First Contact

The first touch with a stranger can frequently revel in intimidating within the location of social interactions. Whether you're at a networking event, a party, or absolutely meeting someone new for your each day lifestyles, the preliminary few moments of discussion can set the tone for the relaxation of the interaction. Breaking the ice is extra than virtually polite pleasantries; it is about growing a cushty and appealing surroundings that fosters actual communique. In this chapter, we are able to take a look at the way to start conversations with any luck, go with the flow beyond clichéd starting comments, and expand at once connection with strangers.

2.1 Hello, Stranger: How to Begin Conversations Confidently

Even the maximum extroverted people can get fearful virtually considering drawing near a stranger and striking up a conversation. Fear of rejection, uncertainty about how you will be dealt with, and the pressure to create an superb effect can all make a contribution to tension. It's important to don't forget, however, that the ability to without trouble start a communication is a capability that can be cultivated and polished with time.

Confidence is Essential

Confidence is crucial for effectively breaking the ice. It's now not about being the loudest or maximum outspoken individual in the room; it's far about being snug on your very very own pores and skin and exuding self belief. Confidence can be superior via exercise and an adjustment in wondering.

Mindset Shift

Fear of rejection is one of the most fundamental barriers to beginning a dialogue with self perception. To conquer this phobia, you have to shift your attitude. Instead of viewing every conversation as a make-or-break opportunity, don't forget it as a chance to observe and join. Although not every interplay will result in a profound connection, every one is an possibility to enhance your skills.

The Nonverbal Communication Advantage

Your body language communicates volumes earlier than you are saying a few aspect. Maintaining open and welcoming body language can communicate to humans which you are approachable and friendly. Maintain proper eye contact, smile, and stand or sit down down in a comfortable but alert posture. These nonverbal cues can help make the preliminary meeting lots plenty less daunting.

Practice Makes Perfect

As with any ability, repetition is critical. Try beginning discussions with strangers in low-risk situations, together with a coffee preserve or while ready in line. The extra you exercise, the greater cushty you may sense and the a whole lot less intimidating it's going to experience.

2.2 Away from the Weather: Captivating Opening Lines

"Nice weather in recent times, isn't it?" While this can be many human beings's bypass-to taking off sentence, it regularly ends in crucial and stupid talks. Engaging starting traces, however, can hold close a person's hobby and set the tone for the rest of the communication. Consider the subsequent techniques for growing thrilling openers instead of relying on climate-related small communicate:

Observational Beginners

Make an observation approximately your surroundings or the situation you and your associate are in. In an artwork gallery, for example, you could say, "I couldn't assist however be aware the complex information on this portray." "What are your mind?" Observational openers show which you're paying interest and which you are in reality interested in the surroundings.

Compliments

A actual compliment may be a excellent icebreaker. Compliments approximately someone's beauty or achievements are frequently effective. Like, "I ought to say, your outfit is appreciably elegant," further to "I heard you gave a superb presentation in advance."

common Experiences

If you are at an occasion or collecting, citing a commonplace experience assist you to make a proper away connection. "This is the number one time attending this event," you could say. "Have you visited right here earlier than?" Sharing your not unusual floor might be an incredible gateway into similarly discussion.

Open-Ended Questions

By asking open-ended questions, you urge the opportunity man or woman to tell you extra approximately themselves. Instead of asking certain/no questions, ask questions that call for additonal information. For example, as opposed to asking, "Did you have got an exceptional weekend?" ask, "How did you spend your weekend?"

2.Three Establishing Immediate Rapport with Strangers

The sensation of connection and know-how that develops amongst people at some point of a talk is called rapport. Building short rapport with strangers is a vital abilities which can decorate the leisure and due to this of your encounters. Here are some techniques that will help you assemble rapport proper away:

Active Listening

The middle of rapport improvement is active listening. Give a person all your hobby whilst they may be speaking. While they're speakme, keep away from interrupting or worrying about what you could say next. Show your appreciation for their phrases thru the use of nodding or making use of vocal cues consisting of "I see" or "That's thrilling."

Empathy

Empathy is the capability to understand and percent the feelings of a few specific person. Consider your self in the shoes of each exceptional individual and word the place through their eyes. When you explicit empathy, you establish a dating and hold in mind. You may also want to answer to them saying, "I can accept as genuine with how difficult that have to had been for you."

Discover Shared Interests or Experiences

Discovering shared hobbies or studies can speedy decorate rapport. If you find out a subject remember or enjoy to that you both relate, dig deeper into that topic of debate. It fosters companionship and mutual statistics.

Use Their Name

One of the nicest sounds to someone's ears is their call. During the chat, make an try to do not forget and hire their name. It indicates that you're paying hobby and are invested inside the interplay.

Authenticity

Be genuine to yourself. Authenticity is vital for growing real rapport. Trying to be a person you are not or the use of canned strains may be disastrous. People like sincerity and are extra inclined to connect to the actual you.

Mirror and Match

Establishing rapport can be completed with the useful resource of subtly mirroring the possibility man or woman's body language and conversational styles. Try to in form their pace if they communicate at a slower price. You can embody similar gestures into your speech inside the event that they make use of them. It need to be sensitive and natural, so do not overdo it.

Chapter 9: Dealing With Awkward Silences

Awkward silences in conversations can purpose pain and worry for loads people. Shivers run down one's spine without a doubt considering a verbal exchange coming to a standstill. However, it's miles vital to recognize that awkward silences are a herbal detail of human connection and must no longer be dreaded or averted. In this bankruptcy, we can check the way to attend to awkward silences, how to deal with instances even as you run out of factors to say, and a manner to use nicely-positioned pauses to beautify your small communication abilities.

3.1 The End of Awkward Silence: Conversational Strategies

Awkward silences can appear for lots of motives. They can appear at the same time as every elements in a communication are burdened what to say subsequent. Other times, they will be the fabricated from a topic that has run its route, leaving a clumsy vacancy. Whatever the purpose, proper right here are some guidelines that will help you gracefully exit awkward silences and maintain discussions strolling effortlessly

Listening Actively and Asking Follow-Up Questions

Your simplest weapon in opposition to awkward silences is energetic listening. Follow-up inquiries will routinely rise up at the same time as you're completely involved in what the opportunity man or woman is announcing. If they element out a cutting-edge tour, as an instance, you could inquire about their favored part or what caused them to excursion there.

Recap and precise

If the verbal exchange entails a halt, you could constantly summarize what has been said and unique your mind. This fills the silence on the equal time as concurrently demonstrating your cognizance. "It's charming the way you described your entrepreneurial adventure," through manner of the use of way of instance. I can discover to the troubles you encountered.

Transitions

Changing topics can spoil the stillness. You can accomplish this with the useful resource of putting in place a hyperlink the diverse modern-day state of affairs and a present day-day one. For example, if you're speaking about excursion and it's coming to an quit, you can commentary, "Speaking of exploring new locations, have you ever ever tried adventure sports activities activities sports?"

Use Humor

Humor is an great icebreaker. A lighter shaggy dog story or a hilarious anecdote can help to relieve anxiety and restart the communique. However, hold your purpose marketplace in thoughts and make sure your humor is suitable for the state of affairs.

Silence Isn't Always Uncomfortable

It's important to recognise that no longer all silences are uncomfortable. Taking a minute to contemplate or allowing the communicate to respire can be suitable at times. In more excessive debates, silence also can unique statistics and empathy.

three.2 What to Do When You're Stuck for Words

A regular trouble is strolling out of things to mention in a dialogue, however this does not must be a communication killer. It's vital to understand that silence is not a lousy issue, and that it'd allow the communicate to flow obviously. However, if you locate yourself in a scenario in that you need to hold the communique going, try the following techniques

Shift the Focus

If you experience like you have exhausted the modern problem, recall transferring the point of interest to the other person. Inquire about their pursuits, pastimes, and previous reports.

This not excellent continues the communicate going, but it moreover demonstrates a true interest in them.

Make Use of Open-Ended Questions

Open-ended inquiries are notable communication openers. Questions that begin with "how," "what," "why," or "tell me approximately" elicit longer responses and cause greater in-depth discussions. For example, "What do you enjoy doing for your free time?" or you can "Tell me about your selected tour holiday spot."

Shared Experiences

Think about commonplace evaluations or interests. If you've got already stated something in commonplace, you can pass over it once more from a unique angle or have a study comparable subjects. Shared reviews regularly provide a hundreds of conversational fodder.

Express Curiosity

Showing interest in the one-of-a-kind character's lives, evaluations, or reviews can hold the communique energetic. People revel in sharing their expertise and research, so take note of what they should offer with actual curiosity.

Share Personal Anecdotes

Sharing personal anecdotes or recollections can be an powerful approach to hold the communication continuing. However, make sure your anecdotes are pertinent to the difficulty to hand and do not take over the discourse.

Pause and Reflect

It's fantastic to pause and reflect in some unspecified time in the future of a verbal exchange. This now not great lets you collect your mind, but it can additionally add depth and notion to the talk. Pauses, while used intentionally, may be pretty powerful tools.

three.Three Perfecting the Small Talk Pause

We regularly leave out the importance of properly-positioned pauses in conversations in our stress to fill each 2nd of silence with phrases. Small chat pauses can also have some of abilities, together with letting the alternative man or woman to absorb facts or growing a enjoy of anticipation or emphasis. Let's observe the way to fine the artwork of small chat pauses

Strategic Pauses

Strategic pauses assist spotlight essential factors for your verbal exchange. When addressing a noteworthy success, as an example, you may statement, "I modified into absolutely glad with that achievement." [Pause] It became numerous difficult work."

Reflective Pauses

Pauses can mean which you're considering or reflecting on a few issue. This can assist to decorate the high-quality of your responses. For example, if perplexed approximately your destiny plans, you can reply, "That's a charming query. [Pause] I've been thinking about it loads lately..."

Inviting Pauses

Use pauses to invite the opposite individual to offer extra records. After they have got said a private event, you can statement a few trouble like, "That seems like pretty an adventure." [Pause] What was your most memorable 2d?"

Listening Pauses

Use pauses to reveal which you're being attentive to the alternative character. It demonstrates that you are allowing them to actually precise themselves. A easy nod and pause may want to probable monitor your hobby.

Avoid Overuse

While pauses may be effective, keep away from overusing them to the thing that they become awkward or seem forced. Natural pauses that match the cadence of the speak are greater a fulfillment in massive.

Silence as Comfort

As previously said, silence does no longer constantly need to be crammed. Allowing a touch pause may want to probable every now and then provide you with and the alternative man or woman a chance to accumulate your thoughts and enjoy a second of silence within the verbal exchange.

Finally, overcoming awkward silences in discussions is a skill that may be cultivated and honed. It's crucial to recognize that no longer all silences are inherently awkward, and that they'll now and again be useful. When faced with awkward silences, go through in mind that attentive listening, test-up inquiries, and transitions can all assist keep the communicate moving.

Chapter 10: Exceeding Surface-Level Chatter

Small chat is frequently criticized for being shallow and without depth Under the ground of polite chats about the weather and weekend plans, but, there may be the possibility for huge and desirable dialogues. In this financial disaster, we will test the manner to move beyond ground-degree communication, a manner to make conversations definitely vast, a way to discover private memories, and a way to invite the precise inquiries to go deeper into the hearts and minds of these with whom you communicate.

four.1 Making Conversations Meaningful: Moving from the Superficial to the Substantial

Conversations with which means are the coronary coronary coronary heart and soul of human connection. They permit us to speak our mind, feelings, and evaluations in a manner that fosters comprehension and empathy. Consider the subsequent processes to move past floor-stage chatter

Active Listening

The basis of big talks is energetic listening. It consists of paying attention to the speaker's phrases and indicating which you charge what they will be pronouncing. When you actively concentrate, you try to recognize the underlying emotions and critiques further to pay interest the terms.

Empathy

The ability to apprehend and percent the emotions of a few other character. Empathy is crucial in significant talks. Put yourself in the function of the alternative character, recognize their emotions, and verify their testimonies. Empathy can foster a robust bond.

Vulnerability and Openness

Meaningful talks frequently necessitate a degree of vulnerability and openness. When you are inclined to speak your mind, feelings, and research certainly, the opportunity character is much more likely to do the same. Be open to sharing your very own memories and feelings.

Expressing Interest

Demonstrate actual hobby in the different person's element of view. Inquire approximately their thoughts and feelings with the beneficial aid of asking probing questions. Inform them that you price their critiques and are inclined to learn from them.

Reflective Responses

Rather than answering with favored comments, provide reflective responses that display you've got idea about what the opportunity man or woman has said. For instance, inside the event that they point out a trouble they may be having, you may statement, "I can do not forget that have to be actually hard." "How do you deal with it?"

4.2 Unlocking Personal Stories: Effective Sharing and Listening

Personal reminiscences feature the inspiration for sizeable dialogues. They allow us to interact on a extra private level and proportion our character reviews. Consider the subsequent methods for eliciting non-public tales to your conversations:

Share Authentically

Begin thru sharing your private non-public tale to result in others to do the same. Be real and simple to your storytelling. Sharing personal reviews will allow you switch out to be extra relatable and build believe.

Active Storytelling

Be an energetic storyteller on the same time as sharing personal recollections. Use your terms to paint a easy photograph, include sensory data, and specific the feelings you had for the duration of the stumble upon. Make your target audience experience as even though they were gift with you.

Listening with Intent

When others percentage personal reminiscences, pay attention carefully. Pay hobby no longer most effective to the records, but furthermore to the emotions and points of view expressed inside the story. In order to illustrate your proper interest in gaining knowledge of more, ask examine-up questions.

Create a Safe Space

Create an environment in which human beings experience snug expressing their very very personal reminiscences. Assure them that their reminiscences can be dealt with with dignity and compassion. Avoid passing judgment and criticism, and instead be a supportive listener.

Respecting Boundaries

While non-public memories may be powerful, barriers want to be reputable. Don't press a person if they may be afraid to provide a selected detail or problem depend. Allow them to percentage at their very own velocity and degree of consolation.

Encourage Positive memories

Encourage the sharing of extraordinary stories that cognizance moments of private boom, perseverance, or accomplishment. Positive reminiscences can boost the dialogue and encourage others.

four.Three Dive Deeper through Asking the Right Questions

The capacity to invite the right questions can find out the depths of huge discourse. Insightful dialogues can be sparked with the aid of considerate and open-ended inquiries, allowing you to advantage a profound knowledge of the opportunity individual. Here are a few techniques for asking the right questions if you want to delve deeper

Free-For-All Questions

Begin with open-ended inquiries that elicit a more unique response. Questions that start with "how," "what," "why," or "inform me approximately" elicit more statistics from the alternative person than a easy sure or no. For instance, "What are your maximum loved memories out of your travels?"

Follow-Up inquiries

Actively concentrate to the opposite person's comments and utilize their responses to set off take a look at-up inquiries. For instance, in the event that they factor out a hobby, you may inquire, "How did you get into that hobby?" "What do you want best about it?"

More In-Depth Meaning Questions

Ask inquiries that dive into the why and the way of a person's testimonies to elicit deeper emotions and mind. Introspection is generally advocated with the useful resource of questions which includes "Why is that this critical to you?" "so "How did that revel in have an effect for your outlook?"

Reflective Questions

Use reflective questions to elicit deeper concept from the opportunity individual. You can also need to answer, "Can you proportion a time while you faced a task and how it modified you?" Introspection and self-discovery are introduced about via way of reflective thinking.

Hypothetical Questions

Hypothetical questions can spark innovative thinking and motive innovative discussions. For example, "If you could adventure anywhere in the international right now, in which can you skip and why Hypothetical inquiries can screen goals and dreams.

Silent Pauses for Thought

Allow for silent pauses after asking a probing inquiry to provide the alternative man or woman time to reflect and react. Allow them to way their mind and emotions without rushing them.

Avoid Interrogation

While asking probing questions is essential, chorus from turning the conversation grow to be an interrogation. To hold a pleasant flow, stability difficult queries with lighter subjects.

Exhibit Vulnerability

Asking deeper questions on occasion necessitates vulnerability for your aspect. Sharing your personal mind and emotions about the problem can encourage the other individual to do the equal.

Going beyond floor-degree banter, in give up, is ready having meaningful conversations that expand connection and knowledge. It involves energetic listening, empathy, openness, and the potential to find non-public memories. You might also moreover enhance connections and create memorable conversations via using asking the right questions and fostering deeper discussions. Remember that massive interactions not only make stronger your bonds but moreover allow for private boom and self-discovery. Accept the electricity of these dialogues that will help you assemble greater large and satisfying connections on your lifestyles.

Conversational Maneuvers for Every Stage

Mastering the art work of communique requires greater than certainly information what to mention; it moreover requires understanding how to mention it. In this bankruptcy, we can study the crucial thing verbal tactics that might take your interactions to the subsequent diploma. These abilties are important for all conditions, whether or not you're beginning a conversation, developing thrilling conversations and responses, or trying to keep a person's interest.

5.1 Conversation Skills for Every Situation

Effective verbal exchange abilties are your fee charge ticket to a success interactions in hundreds of situations, whether or not or not it's miles a industrial employer assembly, a social event, or a threat contact with a stranger. These skills aren't restricted to high-quality conditions; they may be adaptable and can be used everywhere. Here are a few useful verbal exchange abilities for any situation

Active Listening

The foundation of any exceptional communication is lively listening. It involves no longer best taking note of the phrases stated however furthermore comprehending the feelings and intentions underlying them. Maintaining eye contact, nodding in settlement, and delivering verbal cues inclusive of "I see," or "Tell me more" display which you are absolutely engaged.

Empathy

The functionality to apprehend and share the emotions of another individual. It is a potential that transcends situations and is vital for connecting people. Empathy creates a strong and supportive environment for the other character to specific themselves.

Adaptability

Effective communicators are adaptable. They can tailor their verbal exchange fashion to their communication accomplice's tastes and degree of comfort. Being adaptable to your technique ensures that you may hook up with a wide spectrum of people.

Clarity and Conciseness

In every communique, easy and concise verbal exchange is crucial. Avoid the usage of jargon or unnecessarily complicated language, and reason to speak your mind sincerely. This no longer simplest guarantees comprehension however additionally indicates attention for the possibility individual's time.

Respectful Disagreement

Disagreements are an inevitable a part of any discourse, and knowledge a manner to manage them properly is a useful capability. Avoid private attacks and as an possibility cope with discussing thoughts or elements of view. It is viable to no longer trust out being unfavourable.

Body Language Awareness

Your nonverbal cues can speak actually as masses as, if not greater than, your phrases. Be aware of your frame language, which incorporates your posture, gestures, and facial expressions. Make sure your nonverbal cues in shape the message you are communicating verbally.

Topic Versatility

Being capable of engage with a diverse form of human beings requires subject matter flexibility. While you could have non-public likes and options, being open to discussing hundreds of subjects will let you become a extra exciting conversationalist.

5.2 Creating Remarkable Dialogues and Reactions

Creating memorable dialogues and responses is a skill that may match away your discussion companions with an extended-lasting effect. These conversations are approximately extra than genuinely the phrases you use; they're about the emotional effect and connection you are making. Here's the way to create such dialogues:

Storytelling

Stories have the unique functionality to fascinate an target audience even as additionally making your idea extra accessible. When narrating a tale, be privy to the factors that elicit emotions and paint a sturdy intellectual photo. Describe factors of interest, sounds, and emotions to interact the senses.

Emotional Appeal

Make an emotional connection with your communique partner. Share private anecdotes or research that illustrate your emotions and vulnerabilities. Emotional sincerity can bring about extra significant connections.

Ask Provocative Questions

Thought-frightening subjects can spark active debates. Pose questions that stimulate perception and research of deeper issues. For instance, "What's one element that you've usually preferred to do however however have now not gotten the risk to?" Such inquiries elicit considerate responses.

Active Engagement

Demonstrate lively engagement through manner of the use of asking comply with-up questions and presenting remarks that exhibit your hobby within the verbal exchange. Instead than clearly nodding, say some problem like, "That's captivating! "Could you please complicated?"

Humor

Humor may be an effective device for growing memorable talk. A nicely-timed comic story or smart remark can lighten the mood and decorate the verbal exchange. However, maintain your intention marketplace in mind and keep away from ugly comedy.

Incorporate Analogies and Metaphors

Analogies and metaphors can help to simplify hard thoughts and make your trouble greater comprehensible. They offer a familiar surroundings that lets in comprehension. For example, "Learning a modern language is just like unlocking a door to a whole new global."

Express thankfulness

Including expressions of thankfulness for your responses may additionally have a awesome impact. Recognizing the alternative character's contributions, whether or no longer it is as smooth as "Thank you for sharing that with me" or a more complicated display of appreciation, can decorate the quality of the conversation.

five.Three The Science of Maintaining People's Interest

It is each an artwork and a technology to hold humans's hobby ultimately of a verbal exchange. Mastering this functionality can set you apart as an exciting communicator in an age of distractions and quick interest spans. Here are severa hobby-technological know-how-based completely without a doubt techniques:

Be Present

Being truly present in the conversation is the maximum efficient method to keep a person's interest. Give the alternative man or woman your whole interest and fight the impulse to test your phone or allow your mind wander.

Maintain Eye Contact

Maintaining eye touch is an powerful technique for retaining interest. It indicates which you are involved and interested by the speak. However, keep away from making the alternative man or woman uncomfortable through using staring.

Variate Your Tone and Pace

Monotone discourse can bore humans. To preserve the communication exciting, exchange your tone, pitch, and pace. To emphasize important facts or emotions, use emphasis.

Use Visual Aids

In a few conversations, seen aids can assist to decorate know-how and hold people's interest. Visual equipment, whether or now not a diagram, a chart, or a easy drawing, can function a visible anchor for the talk.

Tell Interesting Stories

Stories are intrinsically captivating. Make your memories thrilling and exciting just so your talk companion is demanding to pay interest what happens next.

Encourage energetic participation thru asking questions and concerning the opposite individual within the discourse. People are more willing to live engaged after they believe their opinions are reputable.

Chapter 11: Captivating Storytelling Secrets

Storytelling is an age-antique art work shape with the potential to fascinate, inspire, and be a part of people on a deep level. The potential to create fascinating recollections is a precious potential, whether or not you're sharing non-public anecdotes, presenting statistics, or genuinely interesting. In this bankruptcy, we can discover the trends that make a tale compelling, the manner to growth and proportion memories that engage with your target market, and procedures to turn out to be a storytelling seasoned.

6.1 The Elements of a Good Story

Captivating reminiscences have a few vital features that lure in and maintain the aim market's interest. These elements make a contribution to the appearance of a fantastic and first-rate tale experience. Let's take a look at the number one materials of compelling storytelling

Compelling Characters

At the coronary heart of any tale are the characters. They provide the target marketplace with someone to root for, relate to, or be inquisitive about. Characters with intensity, motivations, and flaws are greater relatable and compelling.

Clear environment

A well-defined environment gives the tale mindset. It assists the target audience in visualizing the region wherein the story takes vicinity. A colourful surroundings immerses the goal market in the plot and gives intensity to the narrative.

Involving Plot

The plot is the gathering of sports activities that include the tale. It must be well-established, with an advent, growing movement, climax, declining motion, and resolution. Conflict, depth, and a revel in of reason produce appealing narratives.

Conflict and Resolution

A story's driving pressure is battle. It builds suspense and maintains the target market fascinated. The resolution gives the tale completion and pride. It is not crucial for the selection to be pleased, however it must be essential.

Emotion and Empathy

Emotional stories are more likely to be captivating. A greater connection is formed while the viewer can empathize with the characters and understand their joys, sorrows, and problems.

Themes and Messages

A specific tale often explores normal situation subjects and gives essential messages. Stories with underlying project topics, whether or no longer approximately love, friendship, braveness, or justice, connect with the viewer on a private diploma.

Conflict Resolution

A story's using strain is warfare. It builds suspense and keeps the target marketplace concerned. The decision gives the story final contact and pleasure. It isn't usually crucial for the decision to be glad, but it want to be vital.

Pacing

A tale's pacing determines its impact. A stability of calmer, meditative moments and faster, motion-packed sequences is needed for powerful storytelling. Pacing determines the waft of the tale and maintains the aim market concerned.

Surprise and Suspense

Including unexpected twists or surprises in a tale can growth excitement and suspense. Keeping the target audience on their feet will boom their involvement and hobby.

Visualization

Use remarkable and descriptive language to assist the viewer photo the story's occasions and characters. Describe attractions, sounds, smells, tastes, and textures to interact the senses.

Voice and Tone

The narrator's or characters' voice and tone can also additionally have a considerable effect at the storytelling revel in. Consider the emotion you need to supply—whether or not or now not it's miles funny, despair, motivating, or mysterious—and pick out out out a voice and tone that suits.

6.2 How to Create and Share Resonant Stories

Crafting and handing over memories which are tremendous for your target audience consists of excellent notion and talent. Here are a few strategies and tactics to help you assemble and supply notable narratives

Know Your Audience

It is critical to understand your target market's pastimes, values, and choices. Make your story relevant to their memories and feelings. Think of what's going to capture and have interaction them.

Begin with a Strong Hook

Begin your story with a strong hook that right now draws the audience's hobby. It may be a startling statement, a fascinating inquiry, or an intensive description of the placing.

Create a excellent Structure

Create a extremely good beginning, center, and result in your tale. Establish the warfare, amplify anxiety, then provide selection. A properly-dependent narrative is simple to take a look at and engage with.

Show, Don't Tell

Rather than in reality informing the goal market what is going on, exhibit it with actions, speech, and sensory factors. Allow the target audience to experience as despite the fact that they may be a part of the tale.

Use Dialogue Effectively

Dialogue can convey characters to existence even as additionally transferring the plot along. Use real and compelling language that exhibits the personalities and motivations of the characters. Dialogue in a story need to sound right and serve a purpose.

Increase Suspense and Curiosity

Keep the audience inquisitive about incorporating suspense and curiosity elements. In order to spark the intention market's hobby, provide questions, generate issues, or hint at destiny sports.

Evoke Emotions

Emotionally hook up with the target marketplace with the useful resource of the use of tapping into common emotions like as love, worry, delight, and depression. Emotional resonance is an effective approach for engaging storytelling.

Edit and Revise

Writing an exciting story often necessitates severa drafts and changes. Examine the clarity, timing, and impact of your story. Remove extraneous statistics and improve the tale to make it extra enticing.

Practice Delivery

How you inform your narrative is certainly as important as the problem itself. Experiment along side your storytelling competencies, which include tone, intonation, and pacing. When telling your story, be aware about your frame language and facial expressions.

Feedback and Adaptation

Be open to audience remarks. Their reactions and feedback would probable provide useful records about what works and what desires to be stepped forward in your storytelling. Adapt your approach in reaction to their feedback.

Variety in Stories

Include a brilliant range of memories for your repertory. Share your personal anecdotes, historic stories, fables, and exceptional memories. Having a massive set of stories permits you to connect with some of audiences and times.

6.Three Techniques for Becoming a Master Storyteller

Developing as a storyteller involves strength of mind and effort. It's a functionality that can be polished with workout, and with the right strategies, you may take your storytelling to the subsequent degree. Here are some strategies to help you emerge as a master storyteller

Learn from Great Storytellers

Study the masters of storytelling—authors, filmmakers, and presenters who have enthralled audiences with their stories. Examine what makes their storytelling effective and try to consist of comparable approaches into your very very own.

Read Widely

Reading widely exposes you to severa storytelling patterns, formats, and voices. Investigate wonderful genres and authors to boom your narrative toolkit.

Take Courses and Workshops

Think about taking storytelling instructions or workshops. These can provide useful insights, remarks, and opportunity to exercise your storytelling in a supportive setting.

Regular practice

is critical for turning into a in a role storyteller. Share your reviews with buddies, family, or coworkers, and have a observe their reactions. Practice lets in you to hone your narrative competencies and gather self belief.

Record Yourself

By videotaping your storytelling schooling, you may observe your widely wide-spread average performance and find out areas for growth. Listen to the recordings objectively and make any essential modifications.

Join Storytelling Communities

Participate in on-line and offline storytelling groups and businesses. Engaging with amazing storytellers can convey idea, comments, and collaboration possibilities.

Use Visual Aids

Visual aids can enhance narrative, specifically in shows or public speaking engagements. Consider which includes pictures, slides, or props to complement your narrative and visually hobby the goal marketplace.

Try Different Mediums

Storytelling can take numerous office work, together with written narratives, oral narratives, podcasts, films, and in addition. Play spherical with it.

Establishing a Friendly and Open Environment

Creating a welcoming and open surroundings is essential for effective communique and the formation of lasting connections. In this bankruptcy, we will observe strategies for all at once connecting with people, the usage of welcoming body language and nonverbal clues, and making others experience snug on your presence.

7.1 Making an Immediate Connection with Others

Making connections with others is an critical part of setting up a warm temperature and open tone on your conversations. Here are numerous techniques to help you all at once connect to someone, whether or not you're meeting them for the number one time or reconnecting with an vintage pal

Active Listening

Begin through the use of being attentive to the alternative character. Pay attentive interest to what they're saying and precise actual hobby of their feelings and perspectives. Pose comply with-up questions to suggest your interest.

Discover Common Ground

Look for shared interests, tales, or values with the alternative person. Mentioning identical pastimes or recollections might probable help to set up a right away bond and make the communicate feel greater relatable.

Use Mirroring

Mirroring is a manner in that you lightly mirror the man or woman you're speaking with body language, tone, and pace. This can assist to installation a feel of familiarity and rapport. However, rent mirroring sparingly and keep away from becoming overly glaring.

Share Personal Anecdotes

Sharing personal anecdotes or memories might also assist you turn out to be extra personable and approachable. When you percentage your non-public reports, you urge the possibility person to do the equal. Vulnerability can assist humans connect.

praise and Positivity

Give actual reward and comments this is effective. Recognizing the alternative person's talents, achievements, or contributions can assist to assemble an wonderful and alluring environment.

Smile

A clean smile can speak warm temperature and openness. When you welcome a person with a type smile, it at once places them comfortable and communicates which you're approachable.

Empathize and Validate

Demonstrate empathy thru acknowledging and validating the opposite man or woman's emotions and evaluations. You can say such things as, "I can recognize how tough that need to have been" or "It sounds along side you had a super time."

Be Present

Being honestly present within the second at the same time as talking with a person conveys a robust statement which you admire their employer. Remove any distractions, maintain eye touch, and provide them your whole hobby.

Express Appreciation

Thank the alternative individual for the opportunity to have interaction with them. "It's top notch to appearance you" or "I'm grateful for our conversation" can help to set a nice tone.

7.2 Body Language and Nonverbal Cues to Welcome

Your body language and nonverbal clues play an essential position in organising a pleasing and open tone. These signs would possibly probable speak sincerity, approachability, and a kind manner. Here are some techniques to try:

Maintain Open Posture

Maintain an open and alluring body language. Try no longer to transport your fingers or seem closed off. Instead, undertake an open posture to indicate that you're open to communicate.

Eye Contact

Maintain proper eye touch sooner or later of the interplay. It demonstrates your engagement and hobby in the particular person. However, keep away from making the alternative person uncomfortable through staring.

Gestures of Welcome

Use open-exceeded gestures, nodding in agreement, and leaning barely toward the character you are speakme with to expose welcome and openness.

Smile and face Expressions

One of the maximum inviting face expressions is a proper smile. Throughout the communicate, use appropriate smiles to demonstrate warm temperature and friendliness. Unless the occasion needs for it, keep away from frowning or displaying horrible feelings.

Mirroring and Synchronization

As previously stated, mirroring can assist to collect a experience of connectedness. To increase rapport, mimic the opposite man or woman's body language and pace. But be cautious no longer to overdo it.

Respect Personal Space

Respect the non-public place and limits of others. Allow them sufficient region to experience comfortable at the same time as keeping off getting into their personal region, which might be regarded as intrusive.

Use Touch Appropriately

A mild and terrific contact at the shoulder or handshake can advise warm temperature and friendship in some cultures and events.

However, in phrases of bodily contact, hold in thoughts cultural requirements in addition to individual options.

Keep a Calm Atmosphere

A calm temperament conveys ease and openness. Avoid tight or inflexible frame language, that may offer the have an effect on that you are ugly or protecting. Take deep breaths and continue to be cool in the course of the chat.

Mirror Emotional Expressions

Mirror the opposite man or woman's emotional expressions to demonstrate empathy and information. Share in their excitement in the event that they particular it. Offer consolation and useful resource if they're sad.

7.Three Making Others Feel At Ease in Your Company

It is important to assemble proper connections via the usage of developing an environment wherein others revel in comfortable. These methods can help you make others revel in comfortable in your company, whether or now not you're in a social scenario, a expert context, or a private communique:

Active Listening

Pay interest to what the alternative individual is saying with out interrupting or judging them. Nod, make extremely good seems like "I see," and offer verbal symptoms that you're interested in the talk to illustrate empathy and understanding.

Avoid Interrupting

Interrupting someone who's talking might be seen as impolite and condescending. Allow the alternative person to clearly express oneself in advance than reacting.

Exercise Patience

Be affected character and permit time for the other person to carry their thoughts and feelings. Avoid hurrying the speak or setting pressure on them to speak hastily.

Avoid Judgment

Create a nonjudgmental surroundings wherein the alternative person can percentage their perspectives and reminiscences with out worry of being judged. Avoid making horrible or important feedback, and avoid leaping to conclusions.

Be Supportive

When suitable, provide guide and encouragement. If the other individual goes thru a tough length, suggest your desire to listen and help if critical.

Respect Boundaries

Be privy to the possibility person's limitations and diploma of consolation. If they're reluctant to deal with certain issues or provide sure records, recognize their goals and keep away from pressuring them.

Encourage Them to Express Their self genuinely

Encourage the other man or woman to express themselves real. Let them recognize that their input and evaluations are valued and considerable within the speak.

Use Inclusive Language

Use language that encourages a experience of belonging and reputation. Avoid the usage of awesome language or making statements that can make the alternative character enjoy excluded.

Validate Emotions

Validate the feelings of the alternative man or woman thru acknowledging their emotions and research. You're able to supply, "It's accurate sufficient to sense that manner" further to "I apprehend why you is probably disenchanted."

Chapter 12: Breaking Bad Habits And Improving Communication Skills

Improving your conversational competencies encompass not actually gaining knowledge of what to mention however additionally spotting and fending off regular conversational traps that may stymie first-rate communique. In this financial ruin, we're going to have a take a look at the manner to avoid and overcome the ones issues, similarly to the way to address the diffused dispositions that would keep you again in discussions and domesticate a fascinating presence that improves your interactions.

eight.1 Recognizing and Avoiding Common Conversational Pitfalls

Effective communique includes now not definitely studying new abilties, but moreover spotting and addressing everyday conversational problems that could stymie your conversations. Let's look at some of those dangers and a way to keep away from them

Interrupting

A conventional conversational blunder is interrupting someone at the same time as they're speakme. It has the capability to make the opportunity individual revel in unheard and mistreated. Practice energetic listening and anticipate the speaker to complete before reacting to break this conduct. If you want to express yourself, make a intellectual be aware to go back to them on the same time as it's your turn.

Over-Talking

Dominating a communication through exaggerating your very own or your interests may moreover alienate others. To avoid this entice, maintain the conversation balanced by way of using the usage of asking questions and expressing right hobby in the extraordinary man or woman's issue of view. Keep in mind that talks are a -manner street.

Not Actively Listening

Passive listening, in that you are physical gift but mentally absent, is a not unusual blunder. Focus at the speaker, preserve eye touch, nod in agreement, and offer verbal cues to illustrate you are fascinated to grow to be an energetic listener. Avoid distractions and completely interact within the discourse.

Judgment and Criticism

During a verbal exchange, passing judgment or being overly important can create a adversarial environment. Instead, exercising empathy and comprehension. Allow for specific factors of view and technique dialogues with an open mind.

One-Upping

Constantly striving to outdo others by expressing your very own reviews or accomplishments may be traumatic. Validate the other individual's reviews and contributions alternatively. Show real interest in their stories without in search of to outdo them.

Lack of Empathy

Empathy is a essential factor of appropriate communique. Failure to empathize with the feelings or evaluations of others can cause misunderstandings and strained relationships. Empathy is confirmed through acknowledging their sentiments and indicating that you care approximately their factor of view.

wrong Humor

While humor can enhance talks, incorrect or insulting jokes may be dangerous. Keep your target marketplace in thoughts and avoid any comedy that would offend or upset them. When suitable, bypass for inclusive and lighthearted comedy.

Topic Dominance

Constantly directing the communication closer to your chosen topics or pursuits should make others revel in neglected. Allow human beings to introduce subjects and contribute their thoughts to widen the communique. Be open to your subject matter choice.

8.2 The Inconspicuous Habits That Hold You Back

Aside from the plain conversational troubles, there are diffused conduct and behaviors that could restriction your conversations. Recognizing and solving those behaviors allow you to beautify your speakme talents appreciably:

Self-Doubt

Self-doubt would in all likelihood show itself as reluctance, self-grievance, or a loss of self perception on your communique talents. Practice self-compassion and excessive satisfactory self-communicate to overcome self-doubt. Concentrate in your strengths and feature amusing your achievements.

Negative Self-Talk

Negative self-talk can lower your conceitedness and make it tough to speak.

Positive affirmations want for use to replace awful thoughts. Dispel illogical thoughts and remind yourself of your rate.

Insecurity

Insecurity also can bring about in search of validation from others or evaluating yourself to them all of the time. Set possible goals, have an extremely good time your triumphs, and embody self-popularity to construct self-self perception. Recognize that every body has their very very own set of strengths and flaws.

Fear of Rejection

Being frightened of rejection may want to make you cautious to initiate or participate in conversations. Face your dread of social conditions via way of regularly exposing your self to them and working closer to small chat. Remember that rejection is a natural a part of life and does not define your price.

Rigidity

Being too strict in your ideals or evaluations can also stifle open and healthy speak. Develop your open-mindedness via using way of actively searching out specific elements of view and confronting your very personal biases. Be inclined to exchange your mind in response to clean understanding.

Perfectionism

Trying to be ideal to your talks may in all likelihood cause tension and self-criticism. Accept flaws and recognize that mistakes rise up. Concentrate on how you could take a look at and beautify from your relationships.

Passivity

Avoiding expressing your desires or thoughts via passive communication can stymie effective talks. Practice assertiveness thru the use of expressing your self honestly at the same time as respecting the rights of others. Assertive communique promotes excessive first-class interactions.

Absence of Presence

Being mentally absent for the duration of a communication can degrade its top notch. Combat this via operating in the direction of mindfulness and last in the present second. Avoid distractions and actively interact with the character with whom you're talking.

8.Three Charismatic Presence Development

Charisma is a character trait that can enhance your conversational abilities and make you extra appealing and influential for your interactions. While a few human beings are born with charisma, it is able to additionally be evolved and perfected. Here are a few strategies for cultivating a charismatic presence:

Confidence

A crucial aspect of charisma is self belief. Have religion in yourself and your capability. To express self assurance, stand tall, create eye touch, and rent outstanding frame language. People are attracted to self perception due to the fact it is magnetic.

166

Authenticity

The foundation of air of thriller is authenticity. In your encounters, be real and real to yourself. Avoid pretending to be someone you're not, because authenticity connects with others and creates be given as proper with.

Positive Energy

Charismatic humans emit a number of power and enthusiasm. Develop an awesome mindset and technique interactions with zeal and electricity. Share your enthusiasm and exuberance for the state of affairs accessible.

Active Engagement

Participate clearly for your talks. Demonstrate which you are present and engaged in what the other character is pronouncing. Ask questions, percent your mind, and actively take part within the talk.

Active Listening

Charismatic communicators are identified for their energetic listening abilities. Giving your entire interest to the speaker, asking clarifying questions, and showing empathy and know-how are all examples of lively listening.

Storytelling

Good storytelling can improve your air of secrecy. Create and share tales which can be large on your goal market. To entice your aim marketplace, use vivid data, feelings, and relatable studies.

Humor

When carried out effectively, humor can be a charismatic trait. Use comedy this is suitable for the situation and the tastes of your goal marketplace. Aim for inclusivity and avoid offensive or debatable humor.

Chapter 13: Attracting Genuine Friendships

Friendships are the muse of satisfied lifestyles, and making actual connections with others is a powerful and fulfilling enjoy. In this bankruptcy, we will take a look at the importance of actual connections, the manner to apply small talk to shape extended-lasting bonds, and procedures for increasing your social network and coming across like-minded people.

nine.1 The Influence of Genuine Connections

Genuine ties with others are treasured. They beneficial aid us, decorate our lives, and add to our giant happiness. Here's why right connections are so effective:

Emotional Support

Genuine connections offer a strong emotional useful resource network. Friends that recognize and get hold of you for who you're provide assist at some point of tough times and feature fun your accomplishments.

Shared Experiences

Genuine bonds are shaped via shared recollections, every happy and horrible. These encounters form relationships and memories that growth your bond with others.

Improved Well-Being

Genuine friendships improve your general properly-being. They alleviate loneliness, boom vanity, and create a revel in of belonging.

Increased Happiness

Having sincere relationships to your life results in prolonged happiness and lifestyles pride. Sharing your joys and issues with others enriches your life.

Emotional Development

Genuine interactions sell emotional development and self-hobby. Friends may also additionally provide new mind, challenge your ideals, and help you in becoming a higher model of your self.

9.2 Using Small Talk to Form Long-Lasting Bonds

While small communicate may additionally seem like shallow, it is able to be a crucial approach for building long-lasting friendships and proper connections with others. Here's a manner to make the maximum of small speak

Find Common Ground

Common topics which includes the climate or modern statistics are commonly used to start small speak. Use those problems as a jumping-off issue to discover not unusual pastimes and reviews. Once not unusual ground is diagnosed, the talk can development into deeper, greater widespread talks.

Ask Open-Ended Questions

Rather than asking positive/no questions, ask open-ended inquiries that inspire the opposite person to expose extra approximately themselves. Instead of asking, "Did you've got an wonderful weekend?"

inquire, "What did you do over the weekend that you cherished?"

Exhibit Genuine Interest

Show proper interest within the responses of others. Actively concentrate, ask observe-up questions, and participate inside the discourse with hobby and satisfaction. The conversation receives more relevant whilst you reveal which you are inquisitive about their evaluations and reviews.

Share Personal Anecdotes or Stories

Sharing private anecdotes or stories can help to make small chat more approachable and human. It helps the opportunity person to examine greater approximately you and encourages them to open up in bypass again.

Empathize and Validate

During small communicate, practice empathy by way of acknowledging the alternative man or woman's emotions and reports. If they will let you recognize about a problem they will be having, you may reply some thing like, "I can imagine that must be difficult" or "It seems like you have got had pretty an adventure."

Moving at once to More In-Depth Topics

Once you have got created rapport via mild communicate, do not be scared to move directly to more extreme topics. "I've without a doubt loved our conversation thus far," you could say. "May I ask you a extra personal query?" This shows which you want to move beyond the surface-level discussion.

Listen Actively

Active listening is crucial in each brief talk and deeper conversations. Maintain eye touch, nod, and provide verbal symptoms that you're being attentive to show which you're truly concerned.

Be honest

While small chat frequently includes society conventions and pleasantries, it's miles critical to be honest and proper to yourself. Don't act like someone you're now not or talk troubles that make you uncomfortable. Authentic connections are built on authenticity.

9.Three Creating a Social Network and Meeting Like-Minded People

Building a strong social network and connecting with like-minded people is vital for cultivating proper connections. Here are some techniques for broadening your social circle and connecting with folks who percentage your pastimes and values:

Join Clubs and Groups

Look for golf equipment, companies, or agencies that interest and inspire you. These venues, whether or now not or now not a sports activities sports sports activities membership, a literature membership, or a community provider business enterprise, permit opportunity to satisfy like-minded humans.

Attend Events and Workshops

Go to activities, workshops, and lectures to your hobbies or pursuits. These activities regularly appeal to others who percent your ardour and might motive precious connections.

Utilize Social Media

Social media systems may be useful for connecting with others who percent your interests. Participate in on-line groups, boards, or companies devoted in your pastimes. Participate in discussions, make a contribution your know-how, and make connections with individuals who percent your beliefs.

Volunteer

Volunteering is a extraordinary way to fulfill folks that care about the same property you do. Whether you are walking for a community charity, an environmental organisation, or a network initiative, you will almost in fact meet others who share your preference to make a difference.

Networking Events

Attend networking activities related to your career or organization. These activities allow you to network with experts who proportion your professional pastimes and pursuits.

Take Classes

Enroll in lessons or publications which are related to your pursuits or activity dreams. You'll meet others who percentage your pursuits, whether or no longer it's far getting to know a new language, taking a cooking class, or obtaining a certification.

Utilize Online Platforms

Online platforms that hyperlink human beings based totally on shared pursuits may be extensive sources. Meetup, Eventbrite, and expert social networks assist you to discover activities and companies which can be focused in your selections.

Ask for Introductions

Don't be afraid to invite buddies and pals if they're able to placed you in contact with like-minded human beings they realize. Mutual ties have to make the device of forming new partnerships much less difficult.

Be Open-Minded

While looking for like-minded humans, be open to meeting human beings with unique views and backgrounds. Unexpected contacts can now and again purpose the most enriching and proper friendships.

Start Conversations

Take the initiative to strike up a communication with human beings you meet in a number of contexts. Initiating a speak, whether or not or not at a social event, a convention, or a network espresso keep, may be step one in forming a connection.

The Influence of Small Talk on Your Life

Small chat, that is often undervalued, has the ability to have a notable impact in your personal and expert life. In this economic disaster, we are going to have a have a look at how regular conversations may be success gatekeepers, a manner to use small talk as an underutilized superpower, and mind for gaining knowledge of verbal exchange methods so you in no manner run out of things to say.

10.1 The Success Gatekeeper: How Simple Conversations Can Change Everything

Small communication is normally left out as idle banter, however it's miles the important factor to achievement in lots of areas of life. Here's how clean talks can modify your life:

Networking and Professional Advancement

Small communique is essential for networking and task boom. Through casual chats, you can construct rapport with coworkers, superiors, and business enterprise peers, which could bring about new possibilities, partnerships, and mentorship.

First Impressions

When meeting new human beings, small communication is generally the primary factor of contact. The first impressions you are making will have a long-time period impact on your relationships and future interactions.

Professional Relationships

Effective communication is needed for the improvement of best expert relationships. Small communique permits you to hook up with coworkers and customers, selling a wholesome paintings surroundings and growing productivity.

Social Connections

Small conversation allows you to hook up with others on a non-public degree in social activities. These relationships can bring about lengthy-lasting friendships, non-public improvement, and shared stories.

Conflict Resolution

Small chat also can be used to solve conflicts. It allows you to deal with issues, clear up misunderstandings, and restore concord in both non-public and professional relationships.

Negotiation and Persuasion

Small verbal exchange can spoil the ice and installation a great temper in negotiations and persuasion. Establishing rapport with the opposite celebration via casual chat can make them extra receptive on your mind and hints.

Establishing Trust

The basis of any a hit dating is accept as true with. Small chat contributes to the improvement of bear in thoughts via showing your honesty, active listening, and actual hobby in human beings.

Cultural Sensitivity

Small chat can bridge cultural divides and boom records in a globalized society. Understanding and honoring severa cultural conventions in conversation is essential for a success bypass-cultural encounters.

10.2 Unleash Your Underappreciated Power

Small chat, that is often disregarded as trivial, is truly an underutilized superpower that would have a fantastic effect in your lifestyles. Here's the way to efficiently use this superpower:

Active Listening

Use lively listening abilties within the route of quick talk. Show real hobby in what the opposite person is pronouncing, and minimize distractions via asking comply with-up questions. Paying near hobby permits you to attach greater in detail.

Empathy

Practice empathy through imagining yourself in the footwear of others. Attempt to realize their feelings, evaluations, and reviews. Empathy expressed in small chat aids in the formation of substantial bonds.

Body Language

Pay hobby on your non-public and the character you're talking with frame language. Maintain an open and inviting posture, create eye contact, and lease warm and thrilling gestures.

Smile

A smooth smile can be an effective technique in small chat. It conveys friendliness, approachability, and optimism. A kind grin may help to set a fine tone for the communicate.

Find Common Ground

In small speak, look for not unusual floor or shared hobbies. Identifying trouble topics or situations to which you every relate will let you assemble a connection and rapport.

Be Honest

Honesty is essential for unlocking your small speak superpower. Maintain your authenticity on the same time as fending off pretension.

Authenticity builds remember and enriches your conversations.

Express thank you

In small talk, specific thanks with the useful resource of acknowledging the other man or woman's time and communication. A smooth "Thank you for sharing" or "I apprehend your insights" can go an prolonged manner toward installing a first-rate interaction.

Start Conversations

Don't appearance earlier to humans to strike up a communique. Take the initiative to initiate conversations in numerous venues, which incorporates work, social gatherings, and networking sports. Starting discussions indicates self assurance and approachability.

Be a Good Storyteller

Storytelling is an vital capability to have in small chat. Share anecdotes which is probably each appealing and relatable for your target market. Stories which are properly-suggested make you extra exciting and unforgettable.

10.Three Never Run Out of Things to Say: Conversation Techniques

It is essential to master communication skills that allows you to by no means run out of things to say in small talk. Here are some suggestions to help your interactions cross smoothly:

Prepare subjects

Before making small speak, do not forget a few favored topics or questions to make use of as communique starters. Recent opinions, journey, pastimes, or present day-day activities can all be blanketed.

www.ingramcontent.com/pod-product-compliance
Lightning Source LLC
Chambersburg PA
CBHW071340120626

46546CB00002B/631